I BELIEVE
IN
VISIONS

KENNETH E. HAGIN

I BELIEVE IN VISIONS

The fascinating personal story
of a man whose life and ministry
were dramaticaly influenced
by visions of Jesus.

Unless otherwise indicated, all scripture quotations are taken from the *King James Version* of the Bible. Public domain.

29 28 27 26 25 24 23   30 29 28 27 26 25 24

I Believe in Visions
ISBN-13: 978-0-89276-508-9
ISBN-10: 0-89276-508-9

Copyright © 1972, 1984 Rhema Bible Church
AKA Kenneth Hagin Ministries, Inc.
First edition 1972. Second edition 1984.
Printed in the USA

In the U.S. write:
Kenneth Hagin Ministries
P.O. Box 50126
Tulsa, OK 74150-0126
1-888-28-FAITH
rhema.org

In Canada write:
Kenneth Hagin Ministries of Canada
P.O. Box 335, Station D
Etobicoke (Toronto), Ontario
Canada M9A 4X3
1-866-70-RHEMA
rhemacanada.org

Contents

Preface

This book does not contain all the visions I have received from the Lord; however, it does contain most of the major ones.

Chapter 1

How God Raised Me From a Deathbed

"He is dead," stated the doctor who delivered me. I was born prematurely on August 20, 1917, in a house in the 900 block of East Standifer Street in McKinney, Texas.

My Grandmother Drake, who was present at my birth, later told me there was no sign of life in me. Thinking I was dead, the doctor laid me on the foot of the bed, and he and my grandmother continued to work with my mother, who was in very serious condition. She had been ill for several weeks before I was born.

After about 45 minutes had passed and my mother was doing better, the doctor told my grandmother he was going to go to his office to get some supplies he needed. While he was gone, my grandmother picked me up to carry me out. Suddenly she detected a sign of life in me. She washed me and put a little dress on me, but she had to use a makeshift diaper because the regular kind would have swallowed me. Then she weighed me, and with the little dress and diaper on I weighed slightly more than two pounds.

Today even with our advanced medical knowledge and skill and with the incubators we have for premature babies, the chances are very slight for a baby to survive who weighs less than two pounds. I was born in a day when there were no incubators, and I was born in the home, so my chances of living were almost nonexistent.

'The Baby Is Dead'

After a while the doctor returned, and my grandmother asked him what she should feed the baby.

"The baby is dead," he said. "I examined him earlier."

When she told him I was alive and that she had washed and dressed me, he reached into his pocket for a sample package of baby formula. "Feed this to him," he said. "It will last longer than he will."

Granny mixed the baby formula and fed it to me. After that was all gone, she gave me milk, feeding it to me a drop at a time with an eye dropper. She said she had never seen anyone so tiny—she had a large comb that was no longer than I was. She said sometimes even a single drop of milk in my mouth would choke me, causing me to strangle and turn blue.

My childhood was not like other children's, for I had been born with a deformed heart and was not able to lead a normal, active life. I wasn't completely incapacitated, but my activities were limited. I wasn't able to run and play as other children did.

In those days, children didn't start school until the age of 7. However, I learned to read when I was 6. My brother was already in school, so I read his books. Since I couldn't use my body, I used my mind.

Soon after I started school, I learned that children are prone to take advantage of a weaker child. I guess they think that proves how big they are. I couldn't fight to defend myself because I would lose my breath, turn blue, and almost pass out, so I decided I would have to have an equalizer.

There was one boy in our class who was the bully of the playground. He was three years older than the rest of us because he had failed three grades. He would run up to someone and knock him or her down. Knowing I couldn't fight, he seemed to delight in picking on me. One day I found a two-by-four that was about 20 inches long.

The next time he hit me, I got the two-by-four, slipped up on him, and knocked him in the head. He was out cold for 40 minutes. He soon learned to leave me alone. (When a person can't fight, he has to learn to take care of himself some way—and I had.) My older brother learned not to fight with me, either, for I knocked him in the head with a hammer once, and he was unconscious for 45 minutes!

During the years when I was growing up, I was always very small for my age. My brother would tell me I would never be any bigger than a 56-year-old man we knew who weighed only 89 pounds and was the size of a 10-year-old boy. When my brother wanted me to do something for him, he would say that if I didn't do it, I would turn into a girl when I was 12 years old. Of course, he was always about half a block away and running when he said that, because he knew I would hit him with anything I could get my hands on!

My father left Momma and us children when I was still very young, leaving her with all the responsibility for providing and caring for us. When I was 9 years old I went to live with Momma's parents, because Momma's health was very poor and she needed help in taking care of us.

Bedfast at Age 15

At the age of 15, just four months before my 16th birthday, I became totally bedfast. Five doctors, including one who had practiced at the Mayo Clinic, were on my case. My Grandfather Drake, although not a wealthy man, was a man of some means. He had quite a bit of property, although this was during the days of the Great Depression when property wasn't worth too much. If the doctors at the Mayo Clinic had been able to help me, he would have sent me there.

However, my doctors said that the doctor who had been at the Mayo Clinic was one of the best doctors in America. And if he said nothing could be done, it would be a waste of time and money for me to make the trip to the Mayo Clinic.

So all the doctors agreed. They said there was absolutely no hope for me; I didn't have one chance in a million of living. As far as medical science was concerned, to their knowledge, no one in my condition had ever lived past 16 years of age.

Day after day and week after week I lay on the bed of sickness, wondering what was wrong with me. I knew something was wrong with my heart, but I didn't know exactly what it was, because the doctors didn't tell me. Later I learned that I had two serious organic heart problems.

My body became partially paralyzed. I can remember seeing a glass of water beside my bed, wanting to drink it, and not understanding why I couldn't get it. After strict concentration of all my mental powers on it for 45 minutes, I would be able to reach my hand over to it, but I couldn't pick the glass up. One of the doctors said I was bordering on total paralysis and eventually would become completely paralyzed.

Sometimes three weeks would pass when I didn't know anything. My mother and grandmother fed and cared for me, for I was as helpless as a baby. I reached the point where I could hardly hear them talking to me. They later told me that they would put their mouths down to my ear and shout at the top of their voices, but I could barely hear them. It seemed as if they were a block away. I was somewhere between reality and unreality.

I was born and raised Southern Baptist, but I had never been born again. You know, friends, you can be a church member and not be a Christian.

Even though you are a member of a church, that won't save you any more than going to the barn will make you a cow! Being a member of a church won't make you a Christian any more than being a member of a country club will make you a Christian. You have to be born again!

We've got too many people who think they are a Christian just because they are a member of a church.

I joined the church when I was 9 years old. I joined the church because my Sunday School teacher said to all of us boys one Sunday morning, "How many of you want to go to heaven?" Well, every one of us wanted to go to Heaven. So the Sunday School teacher said, "When the pastor gives the invitation to join the church this morning, just go down to the front."

When the invitation was given, since we all wanted to go to Heaven, several of us marched right down to the front of the church and shook hands with the preacher. We joined the church and were baptized in water. And, really, I thought that meant I was a Christian.

Some time later I was in an evangelistic service, and the Spirit of God began to deal with me about being saved—about giving my heart to the Lord. But I reasoned to myself, "But I'm already saved. After all, I belong to a church. I've been baptized in water. I'm already a Christian."

I didn't realize until I had the experience I am about to relate that I had to be born again.

I Went to Hell

I gave my heart to the Lord and was born again the very first night I became bedfast. That was Saturday, April 22, 1933, at 7:40 p.m. in the south bedroom of 405 North College Street in McKinney, Texas.

Earlier that evening before I was born again, my heart had stopped beating, and I died—my spirit left my body.

When death seized my body, my grandmother, my younger brother, and my mother were sitting in the room. I only had time to tell them "goodbye." Then the inner man—my spirit— rushed out of my body and left my body lying dead with eyes set and flesh cold.*

When my Spirit left my body, I went down, down, down until the lights of the earth faded away. I don't mean I fainted—I don't mean I was unconscious. I died. I have proof that I was actually dead. My eyes were set, my heart had stopped beating, and my pulse had ceased.

The Scriptures tell us about the lost being cast into outer darkness where there is weeping and gnashing of teeth (Matt. 25:30). The farther down I went, the blacker it became, until it was all blackness—I could not have seen my hand if it had been one inch in front of my eyes. And the farther down I went, the hotter and more stifling it became.

Finally, far below me, I could see lights flickering on the walls of the caverns of the damned. The lights were caused by the fires of hell. The giant, white-crested orb of flame pulled me, drawing me as a magnet draws metal to itself. *I did not want to go into the jaws of hell,* but just as metal jumps to the magnet, my unre- deemed spirit was drawn to that place. I could not take my eyes off of it. The intense heat beat me in the face. Many years have gone by, yet I can see the cavern of hell just as clearly today as I saw it then. It is as fresh in my memory as if it just happened.

I came to the entrance of hell. People ask, "What does the entrance of hell look like?" I cannot describe it, because if I tried, I would need to have something with which to compare it. (Similarly, if a person had never seen a tree in his life, it would be hard to tell him what a tree looks like.)

Coming to the entrance of hell, I paused momentarily, because I did not want to go in. I sensed that one more foot, one more step, one more yard, and I would be gone forever and could not come out of that horrible place!

Upon reaching the bottom of the pit, I became conscious of some kind of spirit being by my side. I had not looked at him, because I could not take my gaze off of the fires of hell. But when I paused, that creature laid his hand on my arm to escort me in.

At that same moment, a Voice spoke from far above the blackness, above the earth, and above the heavens. I didn't know if it was the voice of God, Jesus, an angel, or who it was. I did not see Him, and I do not know what He said, because He did not speak in English; He spoke in some other tongue. (Later, I realized that it was the Voice of God speaking from Heaven.)

When He spoke, His words reverberated throughout the region of the damned, shaking it like a leaf in the wind, and causing the creature to take his hand off my arm.

I did not turn around, but an unseen power, like a suction, pulled me up away from the fire, away from the intense heat, and back into the shadows of the absorbing darkness.

Then I began to ascend until I came to the top of the pit and saw the lights of the earth. I saw my grandparents' home and went through the wall back into my bedroom. It was just as real to me as it was any time I had entered through the door, only my spirit needed no door.

I slipped back into my body as easily as a man slips into his trousers in the morning. I entered back into my body in the same way in which I had gone out—through my mouth.

I began to talk to my grandmother. She said, "Son, I thought you were dead."

My great-grandfather had been a medical doctor, and Granny had worked with him. She later told me, "In days gone by I dressed many people for burial and laid them out. I have had much experience with death, but I learned more about death in dealing with you and your experiences dying than I

ever knew before. You were dead. You had no pulse or heartbeat, and your eyes were set."

'I Am Dying'

"Granny," I said, "I am going again. I am dying. Where is
Momma?"

"Your mother is out on the porch," she replied. And about
that time I heard my mother praying at the top of her voice as
she walked up and down the porch.

"Where is my brother?" I asked.

"He ran next door to call the doctor," Granny answered.

If you're not ready to go, you want somebody with you.
You're afraid! I said, "Granny, don't leave me! Don't leave me!
I'm afraid I'll go while you're gone! I want somebody with me!
Don't leave me!" So she gathered me into her arms again.

I said, "Tell Momma I said goodbye. Tell Momma I love her.
Tell Momma I appreciate everything she has ever done for me
and for all of us. And you tell Momma that I said if I've ever put
a wrinkle on her face, or a gray hair in her head, I'm sorry, and
I ask her to forgive me."

I felt myself slipping. I said, "Granny, I'm going again. You
were a second mother to me when Momma's health failed. I
appreciate you. Now I'm going, and I won't be back this time." I
knew I was dying, unprepared to meet God. I kissed her on the
cheek and said goodbye.

My heart stopped beating for the second time. It's almost as
real to me today, more than half a century later, as it was that
day. I felt the blood cease to circulate. The tips of my toes went
numb—then my feet, ankles, knees, hips, stomach, and heart
became cold and numb. I leaped out of my body and began to
descend: down, down, down. Oh, I know it was just a few sec-
onds, but it seemed like an eternity.

I began to descend again into the darkness until the lights of earth had faded. Down below, the same experience occurred. Again I stepped to the brink of hell itself and again the Voice spoke from Heaven and again my spirit came up out of that place—back into my room and back into my body. The only difference this time was that I came up from that dark place through the floor at the foot of the bed.

I began to talk to Granny again. I said, "I will not be back this time, Granny." I asked, "Where is Grandpa? I want to tell Grandpa goodbye."

She said, "Son, you know your Granddad went down to the east part of town to collect rent off of some of his rent houses."

"Oh," I said, "I remember that now. I just forgot momentarily."

I said, "Granny, tell Grandpa goodbye. I've never known what it means to have a daddy. He's been the nearest to a daddy I've ever known. He gave me a home when I had none. Tell him I appreciate him. Tell him I love him. Tell Grandpa that I said goodbye."

Then I left a word for my sister and two brothers, and my heart stopped for the third time. I could feel the circulation as it cut off again—and I leaped out of my body and began to descend.

Until this time, I had thought, "This is not happening to me. This is just a hallucination. It can't be real!"

But now I thought, "This is the third time. I won't come back this time!" Darkness encompassed me round about, darker than any night man has ever seen.

The Horrors of Hell

I wish I had adequate words to describe the horrors of hell. People go through this life so complacently, so unconcerned, as if they will not have to face hell. But God's Word and my own personal experience tell me differently. I know what it is to be unconscious—it is black when you are unconscious—but there is no blackness to compare with the outer darkness of hell (Matt. 8:12).

As I began to descend in the darkness this third time, my spirit cried out, "God, I belong to a church! I've been baptized in water!" I waited for Him to answer, but no answer came—only the echo of my own voice as it came back to mock me.

It will take more than church membership—it will take more than being baptized in water—to miss hell and make Heaven. Jesus said, *"Ye must be born again"* (John 3:7).

Certainly I believe in being baptized in water—but only after a person is born again. Certainly I believe in joining a Bible-based church—but a person will certainly benefit more from church after he is born again. If you merely join a church and are baptized in water without being born again, you will go to hell!

The second time I cried a little louder, "God! I belong to a church! I've been baptized in water!" Again I waited for an answer, but there was no answer, only the echo of my own voice through the darkness.

It would frighten a congregation out of their wits if I ever imitated the way I screamed the third time, although, if I could scare them out of hell and into Heaven, I'd do it! I literally screamed, "GOD! GOD! I BELONG TO A CHURCH! I'VE BEEN BAPTIZED IN WATER!" And all I heard was the echo of my own voice.

I came again to the bottom of that dark pit. Again I could feel the heat as it beat against my face. Again I approached the entrance, the very gates of hell itself. That creature took me by the arm. I intended to put up a fight if I could to keep from going in. But I only managed to slow down my descent just a little, and he took me by the arm.

Thank God that Voice spoke. At the time I didn't know who it was—I didn't see anybody—I just heard the Voice. I don't know what He said, but whatever He said, that place shook; it just trembled. And that creature took his hand off my arm.

When the Voice spoke, it was just as if there was a suction to my back parts. It pulled me back, away from the entrance to hell, until I stood in the shadows. Then it pulled me up head-first.

As I was going up through the darkness, I began to pray. My spirit, the man who lives inside this physical body, is an eternal being, a spirit man. I began to pray, "O God! I come to You in the Name of the Lord Jesus Christ. I ask You to forgive me of my sins and to cleanse me from all sin."

This time I came up from the pit of hell into my bedroom beside the bed. The difference between the three experiences was that I came up on the porch the first time; I came up at the foot of the bed the second time; and I came up right beside the bed the third time.

When I got inside my body, my physical voice picked up and continued my prayer right in the middle of the sentence. I was already praying out of my spirit.

Now we didn't have all the automobiles in 1933 that we have today—that was in the days of the Depression. But they tell me that between me and Momma praying so loud, traffic was lined up for two blocks on either side of our house! They heard me praying from inside the house, and they heard my mother as she walked the porch praying at the top of her voice.

When I said that prayer asking Jesus to save me, I looked at the clock and saw it was 20 minutes before eight o'clock. That was the very hour I was born again due to the mercy of God because I asked Jesus Christ to be my Savior and save me from my sins. (Rom. 10:9,10).

The instant I was born again, I felt wonderful. It was just like a two-ton weight had rolled off of my chest. I was rejoicing and was happy in my spirit—although I felt wonderful spiritually, I felt no better physically. I was still bedfast. The doctors had been called, and they told my family that I was going to die. I thought I would die that night, but it no longer bothered me. I knew I was ready to go.

My experience of being brought back from the dead is not new. Jesus raised three people from the dead: Lazarus, Jairus' daughter, and the widow's son. The Apostle Peter raised Dorcas from the dead; the Apostle Paul raised a young man from the dead; and others throughout Church history have had similar experiences.

The Best Thing in the World

Through my experience, God brought me to a knowledge of salvation, which is the best thing in the world to know. I was so thankful to know that my heart was right with God, and to know that if I should die before morning I would go to be with Him.

Every night when the lights were out and my family was in bed, I was left alone with my thoughts. I did a lot of thinking and praying. I remember thanking God that I was saved and that I was His child.

I told the Lord I was going to go to sleep smiling and praising Him, and if I should die during the night, they would find me with a smile on my face because I had a praise in my heart. While praising the Lord, I would drift off to sleep. I never had to take anything to help me sleep, and this is still true today.

The Bible tells us that God *"giveth his beloved sleep"* (Ps. 127:2). I am His beloved, as is every Christian, so we can simply take that verse, thank Him for it, and go to sleep peacefully. We don't need tranquilizers or sleeping pills.

The next morning I was awakened by the sun streaming across my bed. The first thing I did was to praise God. I thanked Him for the light of another day. I thanked Him for the sun, trees, flowers, grass, and leaves. I thanked Him for the songs the birds sang. I praised Him for all of these little things that are so wonderful, marvelous, and beautiful.

I had never heard anyone praise God like this, but when one's heart is in tune with God and he knows he is ready for Heaven, there is an automatic praise in his soul. I didn't know anything about divine healing. I didn't know that God answered that kind of prayer. But I thanked God that I didn't die and go to hell!

At noon when Granny would bring my lunch to me on a tray, I would pray and thank God for the food. Then I would say, "Lord, I guess I won't be here by the time the evening shadows fall. I'll probably slip away this afternoon. But I'm so glad I am saved! I'm so glad You didn't let me die and go to hell! I'm so glad I didn't have to stay down there!"

After a while, evening would come, and soon I would be alone in the dark once more. Again I would praise the Lord for salvation. I would tell Him that I probably would pass away during the night, but I was thankful to be saved and ready to meet Him. I would go to sleep smiling and praising the Lord. Day after day, week after week, month after month I did this.

In the fall of that year, when the weather became cooler, I began to feel somewhat better. Granny would prop me up in bed. Then she would bring her Bible to me and prop it up in front of me. I often say that I was a Baptist boy reading my grandmother's "Methodist" Bible.

When I first started reading the Bible I could read only 10 minutes at a time—I couldn't see after that. The next day I would read for another 10 or 15 minutes. After a few weeks of reading this way, I could read for an hour at a time. Finally I could read for as long as I liked.

I had been brought up in Sunday School. I can't remember the first time I went to church, nor can I remember the first time I ever read the Bible. It seems, too, that I have prayed all my life. But until that Saturday night when God permitted me to have a glimpse of hell and I gave my heart to Jesus, I had never really been born again.

You can be religious and be a church goer and not be a born-again child of God. When you are born again, however, the same Bible you have been reading all your life suddenly looks different. As I read Granny's Bible, I found that Jesus Christ is the same yesterday, today, and forever.

The doctors said that I could die at any time, so when I began reading the Bible I began with the New Testament. I reasoned, *I have to utilize this 10 minutes, or whatever time I have, so I will start with the New Testament.*

The Verse That Changed My Life

I read through the Book of Matthew and began reading in the Book of Mark. There I read a verse that was to transform my life: *"Therefore I say unto you, What things soever ye desire, when ye pray, believe that ye receive them, and ye shall have them"* (Mark 11:24).

Salvation is, of course, the most important thing that can happen to a person. But you cannot possibly understand the all-consuming desire a person can have for health, healing, and life when he has never had a normal childhood, has been sick all of his life, and then lies bedfast month after month, knowing that before long this will be his deathbed.

The greatest desire of my heart was to be well and strong. And here in this verse of Scripture Jesus said, *"What things soever ye desire, when ye pray, believe that ye receive them, and ye shall have them."* When I read that Scripture, it seemed as if someone had turned on a bright light in a very dark room. And you cannot imagine how dark it can be even in the daytime, when you are shut in between four walls and are staring at the ceiling day after day, month after month all the time with a feeling of utter hopelessness.

I didn't know that the Psalmist had said, *"Thy word is a lamp unto my feet, and a light unto my path"* (Ps. 119:105). But without knowing the Word, I had that experience. The whole room suddenly seemed engulfed in light, and there seemed to be light on the inside of me. I have never forgotten that experience or that Scripture. It's as if that Scripture were branded on my heart.

Naturally, the devil was right there to plant doubt in my heart. The minute the light came, he came too. But I didn't know at the time that it was the devil. I didn't have enough spiritual discernment or knowledge of the Word to know that.

Subtly the thought came that maybe the words "what things soever ye desire" didn't apply to physical things, but just to spiritual things. Maybe it just meant "what things soever ye desire" spiritually.

When that thought came, the light went out. Doubt had blown out the candle of faith, and I was in the dark again. I believed what the devil had told me, and again I thought there was no hope. I thought I had to die!

I decided to send for my pastor and ask him exactly what Mark 11:24 meant. Looking back now, I see how foolish it was to send for someone to ask if Jesus really told the truth or not! But this was all so new to me, and up until this time I had great confidence in my pastor. I would have believed anything he told me. I was just like so many other people who are following men and not really following God and His Word.

Live by the Word

I try to tell people whom I minister to not to believe something just because I say it. That doesn't make it so. If I cannot prove by the Bible that what I am saying is truth, then don't believe it. Don't accept it. I have no right to force any of my theories or pet doctrines on someone else. I would not want to

impose any of my convictions on others. Let us each live by the
Word of God.

Longing to talk to my pastor about this scripture, I called
Granny to my bedside and asked her to go get the pastor, who
lived about four blocks from our house. She walked to the parsonage, asked to see the pastor and told him that I wanted
him to come to see me. He said he was very busy that day, but
he would come two days later. Granny suggested that he come
early in the morning, because I was more rested and alert in
the morning than later in the day. (After about 10 o'clock in the
morning, I usually lay in a stupor for the rest of the day.) He
said he would come about 8:30 in the morning.

During the years before I became bedfast, I had been very
faithful in attending Sunday School. I never had missed. Yet
in all the time I had been sick, the pastor had not been to see
me once.

When Thursday morning came, the day appointed for his
visit, I eagerly looked forward to seeing him and asking him
the questions that burned on my heart. Eight-thirty came and
went. Nine o'clock came, and I looked anxiously for my pastor.
Nine-thirty, then ten o'clock, but still no word from him. And
even though I lay on that bed for another entire year, he never
did come to see me.

Although I was crushed with disappointment and disillu-
sionment at the time, I could look back later and see that it was
best that the pastor did not come, for he would have told me
the wrong thing. Rather than inspiring my faith to believe God
for my physical healing, he simply would have reinforced the
doubts I already had.

When my pastor didn't come to see me, my grandmother
walked to another part of town to see yet another preacher in
whom she had great confidence. She told him about my condition, and that I had asked to see a preacher. He told her that
he would come, but he, too, failed to keep his promise. Again I

cried with disappointment when he did not arrive, but again it really was a blessing that he didn't come. (Many things we cry about are for our own good, but we don't realize it at the time. We wouldn't be crying if we could just see into the future.)

My aunt, who was a member of another church, said *her* pastor would come to see me. However, by this time I was certain that he, too, would not come. My aunt was superintendent of the Junior Department in the Sunday School of her church. During the years I was eligible to be in her department, when I was 9 through 11 years of age, I went to Sunday School with her and had never missed a Sunday. I had met her pastor, of course.

Job's Comforter Arrives

One day I heard someone knocking on the front door. A member of my family answered the door, and the minute I heard the voice of the caller, I recognized it as the voice of my aunt's pastor. Suddenly my heart leaped with joy because I thought I could ask him what this scripture meant. Surely he would know and could clear up this confusion in my mind. I knew if this scripture meant what *I thought* it meant, I was coming off of that deathbed!

At that time only one person at a time was allowed in my room, so the pastor came in alone. I couldn't see him too clearly, until he stooped over me. Then his face came into focus.

Partially paralyzed in my throat and tongue, I could not speak distinctly, and I would say a lot of things backwards. Sometimes it would take me a long time to get my words out. Often I would have to stumble around for 10 minutes before I could ask a question. My brain didn't seem to work right.

I moved my mouth and lips, trying to say something. I tried to call his name. I tried to tell him to get my Bible and turn to Mark 11:24 and tell me what it meant, but I couldn't get the words out. I was just stuttering; I couldn't frame the words.

Before I could say anything, he thought I was unable to talk. He patted my hand and drawled in his professionally pious voice, "Just be patient, my boy. In a few more days *it will ALL be over.*" Then he laid my hand down and left the room.

Although this pastor had prayed no prayer with me, he went into the living room and said a prayer with my family. For some reason, my hearing was very keen at this time, and I could distinctly hear every word he said, although he didn't pray very loudly.

He said, "Heavenly Father, we ask You to bless this dear grandmother and grandfather who are about to be bereaved of their grandson. Prepare their hearts for the dark hour that is about to come upon them."

As I listened to this prayer, I was like the naughty little boy who was being punished by his schoolteacher by having to stand in a corner. He might have been standing up outwardly, but he thought to himself that on the inside he was sitting down. I felt just as rebellious as that little boy.

Although I couldn't speak the words audibly, on the inside of me I was shouting, "I'm not dead yet!" I listened as this pastor continued his prayer. "Bless this dear, brokenhearted mother who is about to lose her son." My mother had had some hope until then, but he robbed her of what hope she had, and she started crying.

Planning My Funeral

After the preacher left, my grandmother came into my room and asked me if it would be all right for this preacher to preach at my funeral, as he was the only one who had come to see me. I agreed that it would be all right.

Granny then asked me what songs I wanted sung at my funeral. I told her I didn't have any favorites. They could sing whatever they wanted. She suggested two or three, and I said they would be all right. Then she asked me about pall bearers.

She suggested some, and I told her they would be all right. My mother asked me if I wanted to be buried in a certain place she mentioned, and I agreed. Then they left my room. Although the sun was still shining brightly outside, it seemed ever so dark in my room.

All of this so stunned me that I lay motionless on my bed for 30 days. I gave up and wanted to die. But after about 30 days, I began to read the Bible again. I still couldn't seem to get away from Mark 11:24: *"What things soever ye desire, when ye pray, believe that ye receive them, and ye shall have them."*

Later in the fall I became bolder. I told the Lord I had sent for two preachers who didn't come. The third came, but I realized that it would have been better if he hadn't.

I told the Lord that when He was on earth, He said, *"What things soever ye desire, when ye pray, believe that ye receive them, and ye shall have them,"* and that I desired to be healed.

I told Him I was going to take Him at His Word: I was going to believe He told the truth, and this verse meant what it said. If the New Testament was true, then I was going to come off this deathbed.

I told Him I was going to live and not die. "If I don't get off this bed, then the Bible isn't so, and I am going to have them take it and throw it in the trash can." I meant business!

I was determined to get up from that bed, but I still didn't know how to act on my faith in that verse of scripture. A person can cry, pray, and do everything he knows to do, but if he doesn't have faith or know how to exercise faith, he will remain the same. Jesus didn't say just to pray. The key word in Mark 11:24 is *believe.*

Feelings vs. Faith

At this time, I didn't fully understand faith. I prayed and prayed, but I didn't get any results. I was sure that God heard me, and I had a good feeling inside me that he'd heard me, yet my heart still wasn't beating normally.

What I didn't know then is that we have to go by faith, not by our feelings. We have to stand on the promises in God's Word and not look at the circumstances surrounding us.

I did improve to the extent that I was able to use my hands. Sometimes Granny would prop me up in bed for a short time. I would reach down and feel my legs. There was no muscle at all, just bone. I was extremely skinny.

I seemed to be making no real headway, and I said, "Lord, I thought You would heal me." I was so sure He had heard me, but I felt no better. I know now that just feeling better after you pray is no sign that God heard you; likewise, feeling no better after you pray is no sign that God *didn't* hear you.

We cannot rely on how we feel. We have to come back to what God's Word says about the matter. For months I struggled this way.

When New Year's Day 1934 rolled around, it was moving day. Grandpa owned several houses in town, and he decided to move into another one of them. He had told the people who were renting this particular house that he wanted it for his own use. When they moved, he had it redecorated, and then we were ready to move in.

When the movers came, they moved the furniture from the other parts of the house first, saving the furniture in my bedroom until last. When they came to move my furniture, an ambulance came and moved me.

While I was riding along in the ambulance, one of the attendants remarked that he had heard I had been in bed for about a year now.

"Nine months, to be exact," I told him. He said that if I felt like it, they would take me for a little ride through the residential areas so I could see the scenery. I was so happy for this chance to see things I had been missing for so many months.

The smallest joys, which we so often take for granted, can bring immense pleasure to one who has been deprived of them for so long.

I was able to move my head to look out the window as they drove slowly through the town. Then the ambulance attendant said, "Son, if you feel up to it, we'll drive down to the square. Since it is a holiday, there probably won't be much traffic, and you might enjoy it." How wonderful, I thought, to get to see that old courthouse again, the stores, and other buildings in this beloved little town of McKinney with its population of 8,000 or 9,000.

I saw the familiar old drugstore on the corner. I saw the J. C. Penney's store. Next to that was the Mode O'Day dress shop and next to that was Woolworth's. On down was a shoe store and on the next corner a ladies' ready-to-wear shop. Then we turned to go down the south side of the square. I drank in all of these sights, not knowing when, if ever, I might see them again.

Just as we turned the corner and started down the south side of the square, I turned and looked at the old courthouse that sat in the middle of the square. I shall never forget that moment as long as I live. In that instant something said to me, "Well, you never thought you would ever see these old buildings again. And you wouldn't have, if it hadn't been for the kindness of this man who is taking you."

One Gleam of Light

Then I remembered the verse in Mark 11:24: *"What things soever ye desire, when ye pray, believe that ye receive them, and ye shall have them,"* and I recalled the verse that went before it which said, *"he shall have whatsoever he saith."*

As I said it in that ambulance that day, tears rolled down my face. I didn't understand all that I know now. I had just one small gleam of light. It was like a little light peeping through a crack in the door, but it was a beginning point for me this first day of January 1934 about two o'clock in the afternoon.

I said, "Yes, I will see these buildings and this courthouse again. I will come and stand in this courthouse square, because Jesus said that what you believe in your heart and say with your mouth shall come to pass." I had committed myself.

January and February went by, and I was still bedfast. March, April, May, June, and July went by. The devil might have said it wasn't working, but I held on to my confession and refused to give up. I kept telling the Lord that I was going to hold on, that I was standing on His Word, and it had to work!

Finally I saw what I had been doing wrong: *I wasn't really believing what God's Word said. I* was *saying* it in my mind, but I wasn't *believing* it with my heart or *acting* upon what was in my heart.

I realized that for months I had been hoping I would grow better gradually. I was praying with *hope,* not *faith,* and that won't get the job done.

I realized that my faith was not yet based on what God's Word said, but only on what I could see and feel. I could *feel* that my heart wasn't beating right yet. I often would *look* at my legs and arms and start crying because they were unchanged. *I was believing only what I could see with my physical eyes.*

Thus I came to the second week of August 1934. That Tuesday I prayed through the early morning hours. At the usual time my mother came in and helped me with my bath. It was about 8:30 when she left the room. I continued to pray.

My Struggle With Mark 11:24

I had been struggling with Mark 11:24 for a long time, but I still wasn't any better. I told the Lord, "You said when You were on earth that *'what things soever ye desire, when ye pray, believe that ye receive them, and ye shall have them.'* I desire to be healed, and I believe. If You were to stand here in my room and I could see You with my physical eyes and take ahold of your hand, and if You were to tell me my trouble is that I'm not believing, I would have to say that isn't true. *I am* believing."

Then a voice on the inside of me spoke so clearly it seemed as if someone had spoken audibly: "Yes, you are believing as far as you know, but the last clause of that verse says, *'and ye shall have them.'*"

I believed as much as I knew how to believe, but I didn't know enough. A person cannot pray to get faith. The Bible says that faith comes *"by hearing, and hearing by the Word of God"* (Rom. 10:17). We need knowledge of the Word. When this light of knowledge from the Word comes, faith is *automatically* there.

In this moment, I saw exactly what that verse in Mark 11:24 meant. Until then I was going to wait until I was actually healed before I believed I had received my healing. I was looking at my body and testing my heartbeat to see if I had been healed. But I saw that the verse says you have to believe *when* you pray. The *having* comes after the *believing*. I had been reversing it. I was trying to *have* first and then *believe* second. That is what most people do.

'I See It!'

"I see it. I see it!" I said with joy. "I see what I've got to do, Lord. I've got to believe that my heart is well while I'm still lying here on this bed, and while my heart is not beating right. I've got to believe that my paralysis is gone while I'm still lying here helpless, flat on my back.

"I believe in my heart that You have heard my prayer! I believe that my heart is healed and that my paralysis is gone! I believe in my heart that I have received healing for my body!"

As I said this, the thought came to me, "You're a pretty thing. Just look at you, claiming to be a Christian and now you've started lying. Don't you know the Bible says that all liars will have their part in the lake that burneth with fire and brimstone?"

"I am not a liar," I declared.

"Certainly you are, because you said you are healed and you're not."

"I didn't say that I am healed because I feel like it," I stated. "I'm healed because I believe it. And, devil, if you say I am not, then you are a liar. I am acting on the Word of God. If I am not healed, then Jesus is a liar. Go argue with God about it; don't fuss with me."

With this, the devil left me alone. Then I said, "Thank God, I'm healed." I lifted my hands and praised God.

Momentarily, I started to feel my heart to see if it was beating normally, but I caught myself and stated that I wasn't going by feelings but by faith. I kept saying that my heart was well. I praised the Lord in this manner for about 10 minutes.

Up and Out of Bed

Then the Holy Spirit spoke as an inner witness on the inside of me and said, "You believe you are healed. If you are healed, then you should be up and out of that bed. Well people are up at 10:00 in the morning."

I felt this was right, so I pushed myself up to a sitting position with my hands. Then I reached down, got hold of my feet, and swung them around to the side of the bed. I couldn't feel them, but I could see them. Then I said that I was going to stand and walk.

The devil fought me every inch of the way. He kept telling me that I was a fool. Of course I couldn't walk, he told me over and over again. (As long as the devil can keep us in the *sense* realm, he will defeat us. But if we will stay in the *faith* realm, we will defeat him!)

I got ahold of the bedpost and pulled myself up to a standing position. The room started spinning, for I had been in this bed for 16 months. I closed my eyes, wrapped my arms around the bedpost, and stood there for a few minutes. Finally I opened my eyes and everything had stopped spinning.

I declared I was healed and I was going to walk. Feeling began to return to my legs! It seemed as if two million pins were pricking me because the nerves were being reactivated. I rejoiced because it was so wonderful to have feeling back in those lifeless legs, in spite of the painful prickling sensation. After a short time, the pain left and I felt normal.

Determined now more than ever to walk, I held onto the bedpost and cautiously took a step. Then I took another. Holding onto pieces of furniture, I managed to walk around the room one time.

I told no one of this, but the next morning I got up and did the same thing. That night I asked my mother to bring me some clothes because I was going to get up and go to the breakfast table the next morning. She was shocked, but she did as I asked. On the third morning I got out of bed, dressed myself, walked into the kitchen, and joined my family at the breakfast table. And I've been doing it ever since.

Return to the Courthouse Square

On the second Saturday of August 1934, I walked to the courthouse square. It was crowded downtown, because people always came to town on Saturday to do their shopping. I had to elbow my way through the crowd to get to the outside curb of the square. As I stood there, tears coursed down my face, and I thanked God for His goodness.

I took out my New Testament, which I had brought along with me. I don't know what people thought as they watched me standing on the corner with tears streaming down my face as I opened the New Testament to read, but I didn't care. I had read the Scripture which says, *"Prove all things; hold fast that which is good"* (1 Thess. 5:21). I had proved the verse in Mark 11:24, which I had come to love, and had found it true in my life. I knew that God's Word is true. It is possible to have *"what things soever ye desire"* by right believing in God's Word.

Some time later, a doctor checked my heart and said I no longer had any kind of heart trouble. He said that people with the type of heart condition I had almost never get well. This had to be a real miracle, because now he could find nothing wrong with me.

My Ministry Begins

I soon began my ministry as a young Baptist preacher, and pastored a community church just eight miles from that courthouse square. The first year I pastored, I wore out four pairs of shoes walking to preach. I walked down dusty old roads to preach the Gospel, to tell how Jesus had saved and healed me.

I used to say, "I'll preach from the Red River to the Gulf of Mexico, telling everywhere I go that Jesus saves, heals, and is coming again. And I'll preach it from the Louisiana border to the New Mexico state line." I thought at the time that covering Texas would be covering quite a bit of territory!

Because I believed in divine healing, I began associating with Full Gospel people who also believed and preached divine healing. I liked to go to their services, because I enjoyed the fellowship and hearing others who believed in divine healing made my faith grow stronger.

They also preached about being filled with the Holy Spirit and speaking in other tongues, something I didn't quite understand

or altogether agree with, but I tolerated it in order to have fellowship on the subject of divine healing.

The thing that bothered me the most about their services,
however, was when everyone would pray at once. I wasn't
accustomed to it and I started to say something a time or two
to straighten these people out. Then I heard someone else tell
them, "Don't you know God isn't hard of hearing?"

"He's not nervous, either," they replied.

When they invited believers to pray at the altar, I would go
forward to pray with them, but I would stay as far away from
them as I could, because their praying in unison bothered me. I
would get off in a corner somewhere and pray quietly.

After a while it occurred to me that these people knew about
divine healing and my denomination apparently didn't; therefore, they might know more about the Holy Spirit than I did too.
I decided to read through the Acts of the Apostles to see how the
Early Church prayed.

As I read, I couldn't find one place where they called on Dea-
con Brown or Sister Jones to lead in prayer. I found to my utter
amazement that in the Early Church everybody prayed at once.
*"And being let go, they went to their own company, and reported
all that the chief priests and elders had said unto them. And
when they heard that, they lifted up their voice to God with one
accord"* (Acts 4:23,24).

The thing that cinched it with me was Acts 16, where I
read that Paul and Silas were in jail at midnight. Their backs
were bleeding. Their feet were in stocks. Yet at midnight they
prayed and sang praises to God, *"and the prisoners heard them"*
(Acts 16:25). Until then I had believed in praying to God, but I
believed in being quiet about it. But here I saw that Paul and
Silas weren't quiet, even in jail.

The next time I went to the Full Gospel service and they
invited everyone to the altar to pray, I got right in the middle
of them and lifted my voice just like they did. I felt wonderful

release and freedom in prayer. Jesus said, *"And ye shall know the truth, and the truth shall make you free"* (John 8:32). God's Word is truth, and it will set you free.

'That Tongues Business'

But the subject of the baptism of the Holy Spirit and speaking with other tongues which these Full Gospel people preached was quite another matter. For me that "tongues" business was a bitter pill to swallow. I had been warned against it. But as a fellow down in East Texas had said about going around with these Full Gospel people, "It is like a slippery creek bank. You keep fooling around long enough, and you'll slip in!"

I meditated and thought on the scriptures concerning the Holy Spirit and came to the conclusion that the Full Gospel people were wrong. Tongues weren't necessary; they weren't for us today. A believer could receive this enduement of power without speaking in tongues. That was my own opinion, of course. It certainly wasn't scripture.

I said to the Lord, "These are good people, I know. They are thoroughly saved, and they knew about divine healing when my church didn't. I certainly believe in the Holy Spirit. And I believe in the infilling of the Holy Spirit, the enduement of power from on High. I sense a lack of power in my own life, and I know I need the infilling of the Holy Spirit. And I expect to receive, all right, but I am of the opinion that the tongues don't go along with it and are not for us today."

'What Does the Bible Say?'

Immediately the Lord spoke to my heart. I knew it was the Holy Spirit speaking through the Word. That same still small voice that had brought me off a bed of sickness and into divine healing asked me, "What does the Bible say?"

I quoted the Scripture, *"For the promise is unto you, and to your children, and to all that are afar off, even as many as the Lord our God shall call"* (Acts 2:39).

Then the voice said, "What promise is that?" Acts 2:38 said, *"And ye shall receive the gift of the Holy Ghost."* I said to the Lord, "The reference here, Lord, is to the promise of the gift of the Holy Spirit." Then I hastened to add, "But, Lord, I believe in the Holy Spirit. It is the tongues I am not so sure about."

The Holy Spirit always leads us in line with the Word. The Word and the Spirit agree. I am not in favor of following voices, for a person can go wrong following voices. But we can never go wrong following any voice that leads us to walk in line with the Word of God.

Jesus said, *"he* [the Holy Spirit] *shall receive of mine, and shall shew it unto you"* (John 16:14). And *"he* [the Holy Spirit] *shall not speak of himself."* But thank God, the Holy Spirit does speak: *"But whatsoever he shall hear, that shall he speak"* (v. 13).

The born-again Christian has the Holy Spirit in a measure. That means there is a work of the Holy Spirit in the new birth (John 3:5,6; Rom. 8:16). However, this is not the same as the enduement of power that comes as a result of being *filled* with the Holy Spirit (Acts 2:4). That is called the baptism in the Holy spirit (Acts 1:5).

Then the Lord said to me, "What does Acts 2:4 say?"

I could quote the Scripture, of course. But just because you have a scripture in your mind does not mean that you really know what it says. You have to have the revelation of it in your spirit to really know what the Word of God means.

I quoted, *"And they were all filled with the Holy Ghost, and began to speak with other tongues, as the Spirit gave them utterance."* I got this far and said, "'And they were all filled with the Holy Ghost, and began to sp . . . ' Oh, I see it, I see it! 'They were all filled with the Holy Ghost, and began to speak.' *When*

I get filled with the Holy Spirit, I will begin to speak in other tongues too. Lord, that settles it. I am going down right now to the Full Gospel preacher's house and receive the Holy Spirit!"

I walked over to the parsonage and knocked on the door. I said, "I've come to get the Holy Spirit."

The preacher said, "Wait." From that day until this I have never been able to figure out why anyone would ever tell someone to *wait* to get the Holy Spirit.

Why Tarrying Isn't Necessary

Some people say, "Didn't you read where Jesus told His disciples to tarry, and 'to tarry' means 'to wait'?" Yes, but that is not a formula for receiving the Holy Spirit. If that were the formula for receiving the Holy Spirit, then why take the word "Jerusalem" out of that verse? Jesus said, *"Tarry ye in the city of Jerusalem, until ye be endued with power from on high"* (Luke 24:49). It was just as necessary for that group—the 120—to be in Jerusalem as it was that they wait.

Also, they weren't waiting in the sense of getting ready and preparing themselves to be filled with the Holy Spirit. They were waiting for the Day of Pentecost. The Holy Spirit could not be given until then. If they had been waiting and preparing themselves, the Bible would have read, "When they were ready. . . ." But it reads, *"And when the day of Pentecost was fully come."* (Acts 2:1).

Someone said, "Well, waiting gets you ready to receive the baptism in the Holy spirit." No, it doesn't. Getting saved gets you ready. A fellow down in East Texas said, "I had to take back a pig I had stolen before I could get the Holy Spirit."

That is trying to clean yourself up, but you can't clean yourself up: *"The blood of Jesus Christ his Son cleanseth us from all sin"* (1 John 1:7). If you are bloodwashed, you are ready right now to receive the baptism in the Holy Spirit!

Cornelius and his household were not only saved but were also filled with the Holy Spirit—in almost the same instant (Acts 11:14,15). They didn't have time to get ready. The Holy Spirit fell upon them, and they began to speak with tongues.

If it hadn't been for speaking in tongues, we Gentiles never would have gotten into the Church. The Early Church was strictly a Jewish Church until then. Even Peter himself didn't know that the Gentiles could be saved until he had the vision which is recorded in Acts 10. It astonished the Jews who came with Peter when the Holy Spirit was poured out on the Gentiles: *"For they heard them speak with tongues, and magnify God."* (Acts 10:46).

When I told the Full Gospel pastor, "I have come here to get the Holy Spirit," and he told me to wait, I blurted out, "But it won't take me long to receive."

Because the church was having a revival service that night and it was already six o'clock, he wanted me to wait and seek for the baptism of the Holy Spirit in the service. But I knew I would have to wait until the preliminaries and the preaching were over. It would have been nine o'clock before I could have gotten to the altar, and who wants to wait for a gift?

I have been associated with Full Gospel people for many years now, and in all that time I have never told anyone to wait for the baptism in the Holy Spirit. If people say they want to get saved tonight, you don't say, "Wait and come to church on Sunday and seek for salvation." If someone wants you to pray for their healing, you don't say, "Wait." They want to get healed immediately, especially if they are in pain. Salvation is a gift, healing is a gift, and so is the baptism in the Holy Spirit.

A pastor once said, "I know you can receive the Holy Spirit right away, because we read about it in the Acts of the Apostles. But when you have to wait a long time, the experience means so much more to you. Take me, for instance. It took me three years and six months to get the Holy Spirit. I waited and waited and

tarried and tarried. Now the Holy Spirit really means something to me."

I said, "Well, poor ole Paul didn't know that. I wish you could
have gotten to him and told him about that. He got the Holy
Spirit immediately when Ananias laid hands on him. He didn't
wait, tarry, or seek. But then, all he ever did was write almost
half of the New Testament. Of course, Paul did more singlehand-
edly in his 38 years of ministry than any denomination has done
in 500 years. But if you could have gotten to him and told him
to wait for three years and six months, maybe the Holy Spirit
would have meant something to him."

Seeing my eagerness to receive, the Full Gospel pastor reluc-
tantly said, "Well, come on in, then." I went into the living room
and knelt down in front of a large chair. I closed out everything
around me, shut my eyes, and lifted my hands. No one told me
to do it; I just lifted my hands.

How to Receive a Gift

I said, "Dear Lord, I have come here to receive the Holy
Spirit." I repeated in my prayer what I had just learned from
Acts 2:39 and Acts 2:4. Then I said, "Your Word says that the
Holy Spirit is a gift. Therefore, I realize that the Holy Spirit
is received by faith. I received the gift of salvation by faith. I
received healing for my body by faith. Now I receive the gift You
offer. By faith I receive the baptism in the Holy Spirit."

Let me point out here that the Holy Spirit was given on the
Day of Pentecost, and He has been here ever since. God hasn't
"given" Him to anyone since the Day of Pentecost. Now it is a
matter of our *receiving* Him.

I can't find in the Acts of the Apostles where the disciples
ever asked anyone, "Has God *given* you the Holy Spirit?" I do
read where they asked, "Have you *received* the Holy Spirit?"
Paul didn't ask the Ephesians, "Has God given you the Holy

Spirit?" He said, "Have ye received the Holy Ghost since ye believed?" (Acts 19:2).

The emphasis is not on God's giving, because He has already done that. The emphasis is on man's receiving. In the Scripture, the Word says, *"Therefore being by the right hand of God exalted, and having received of the Father the promise of the Holy Ghost, he hath shed forth this, which ye now see and hear"* (Acts 2:33).

> **ACTS 8:14–15**
>
> 14 Now when the apostles which were at Jerusalem heard that Samaria had received the word of God, they sent unto them Peter and John:
>
> 15 Who, when they were come down, prayed for them, that they might receive the Holy Ghost.

Notice that it says "that they might *receive*." Peter and John didn't pray that God would give the people in Samaria the Holy Spirit. They didn't even pray that God would pour the Holy Spirit out on them; they prayed that they might *receive* the Holy Spirit: "Then laid they their hands on them, and they received the Holy Ghost" (Acts 8:17).

> **ACTS 9:17**
>
> 17 And Ananias went his way, and entered into the house; and putting his hands on him said, Brother Saul, the Lord, even Jesus, that appeared unto thee in the way as thou camest, hath sent me, that thou mightest receive thy sight, and be filled with the Holy Ghost.

Ananias didn't say, "God has sent me to pray for you that He would give you the Holy Ghost." He didn't say, "God has sent me to pray for you that He would pour His Holy Ghost out upon you." Ananias said, *"He sent me, that thou mightest . . . be filled with the Holy Ghost."*

We don't pray that God would *send* salvation and save someone, for God already did that (John 3:16). All a person has to do is *receive the salvation that Jesus already provided for them.* We don't pray that God would *send* healing and heal someone for God already provided healing in the atonement (Isa. 53:4,5; Matt. 8:17; 1 Peter 2:24). We pray that the person would *receive* healing. Neither do we pray that God would send His Spirit to fill a hungry heart; we need only to open our hearts and *receive.*

There in that parsonage in April 1937, I said to the Lord, "The Holy Spirit is a gift. I received salvation by faith. I received healing in my body three years ago by faith. Now I receive the gift of the Holy Spirit by faith. And I want to thank You now because I have received."

Notice that we don't speak in tongues and then know we have the Holy Spirit. We have the Holy Spirit first; *then* we speak in tongues: *"And they were all filled with the Holy Ghost, and began to speak with other tongues, as the Spirit gave them utterance"* (Acts 2:4).

Speaking with other tongues is a result of having received the Holy Spirit. We receive the Holy Spirit first.

I said to the Lord, "I have received the Holy Spirit. He is in me because Jesus promised, 'He shall be in you.' I say it with my mouth because I believe in my heart that I have received the Holy Spirit. Now I expect to speak with tongues because they did on the Day of Pentecost. And, thank God, I will. I have received the Holy Spirit. I believe that. And I will speak with tongues now as the Holy Spirit gives me utterance."

I was grateful for the Holy Spirit whom I had received and for the speaking with tongues that He was going to give me, so I said, "Hallelujah, Hallelujah." But I had never felt so spiritually dry in my life as when I said it.

Feelings and faith are far removed from each other, however, and *sometimes when you feel you have the least faith, that is when you have the most!* So I said, "Hallelujah" seven or eight times, even though I felt so dry spiritually it seemed as if that word would choke me.

Speaking in Tongues!

About the time I had said "Hallelujah" for the eighth time, not very fast, but very slowly—way down inside of me—there were these strange words. It seemed as if they were just going around inside me. It seemed that I would know what they would sound like if they were spoken, so I started speaking them out. And eight minutes after I first knocked on that pastor's door, I was speaking in tongues! He had said, "Wait," but instead of waiting, I spent that hour and a half before the service speaking in tongues.

I believe in waiting on God, of course. We should have "tarrying meetings" for everyone who is Spirit filled. It is more wonderful to tarry and wait filled with the Holy Spirit than without.

During the hour and a half that I was talking in tongues, I had a glorious time in the Lord. Talking in tongues edifies you: *"He that speaketh in an unknown tongue edifieth himself"* (1 Cor. 14:4). This is a spiritual edification, or the building up of one's spirit.

Language students tell us that we have a word in our modern vernacular that is closer to the meaning of the Greek word than "edify," and that is the word "charge." We charge a battery—we build it up. Paul said, *"He that speaketh in an unknown tongue edifieth himself."* He charges himself. He builds himself up like a battery.

After I received the baptism in the Holy Spirit, I continued to preach the same thing I had been preaching; I just added this teaching about the Holy Spirit to it. The Holy Spirit will help a minister enlarge his vision.

My Vision Expands

I had said, "I'll preach that Jesus saves and heals. I'll preach that He fills with the Holy Spirit and that He is coming again. Now I'll preach from the Atlantic Coast to the Pacific Coast. (I even got bigger in my thinking than Texas. The Holy Spirit will make your vision even bigger than Texas!) I'll preach it from Los Angeles to New York. I'll preach it from the Gulf of Mexico to the Canadian border."

And God has blessed my ministry so that I have been able to do it. During the years I was in the field ministry, I traveled more than a million miles throughout the United States and Canada by automobile.

For more than half a century now I have been proclaiming the glorious Gospel of our Lord Jesus Christ, first as a local pastor, then as an evangelist throughout North America, and now internationally as a prophet and teacher.

---

*For a complete account of this experience, see Rev. Hagin's minibook, *I Went to Hell.*

Chapter 2

Come Up Hither

As the Lord continued to deal in my life, He appeared to me in vision form on several occasions.

To understand the scriptural background for visions, let us go back to the Day of Pentecost. Following the mighty outpouring of the Holy Spirit, Peter boldly preached a sermon to those who had gathered to see the marvel of the 120 speaking in other tongues.

A portion of Peter's message to the crowd is found in Acts chapter 2:

ACTS 2:14–21

14 But Peter, standing up with the eleven, lifted up his voice, and said unto them, Ye men of Judaea, and all ye that dwell at Jerusalem, be this known unto you, and hearken to my words:

15 For these are not drunken, as ye suppose, seeing it is but the third hour of the day.

16 But this is that which was spoken by the prophet Joel;

17 And it shall come to pass in the last days, saith God, I will pour out of my Spirit upon all flesh: and your sons and your daughters shall prophesy, and your young men shall see visions, and your old men shall dream dreams:

18 And on my servants and on my handmaidens I will pour out in those days of my Spirit; and they shall prophesy:

19 And I will shew wonders in heaven above, and signs in the earth beneath; blood, and fire, and vapour of smoke:

20 The sun shall be turned into darkness, and the moon into blood, before that great and notable day of the Lord come:

21 And it shall come to pass, that whosoever shall call on the name of the Lord shall be saved.

As the astonished crowd heard the believers speaking in other tongues, *"They were all amazed, and were in doubt, saying one to another, What meaneth this? Others mocking said, These men are full of new wine"* (Acts 2:12,13). But Peter boldly proclaimed, *"This is that which was spoken by the prophet Joel"* (Acts 2:16), and he went on to repeat Joel's prophecy:

JOEL 2:28–32

28 And it shall come to pass afterward, that I will pour out my spirit upon all flesh; and your sons and your daughters shall prophesy, your old men shall dream dreams, your young men shall see visions:

29 And also upon the servants and upon the handmaids in those days will I pour out my spirit.

30 And I will shew wonders in the heavens and in the earth, blood, and fire, and pillars of smoke.

31 The sun shall be turned into darkness, and the moon into blood, before the great and the terrible day of the Lord come.

32 And it shall come to pass, that whosoever shall call on the name of the Lord shall be delivered: for in mount Zion and in Jerusalem shall be deliverance, as the Lord hath said, and in the remnant whom the Lord shall call.

In other words, Peter explained that this manifestation which the people were witnessing had been foretold by God's prophet centuries before. It heralded a new dispensation—a new day of God's grace—and the beginning of the "last days" which Joel referred to. Today we are living in the end of these "last days."

A Young Man's Vision

One of the fulfillments of Joel's prophecy and the outpouring of the Spirit was that *"your young men shall see visions"* (Joel 2:28). *The Amplified Bible* says, *"your young men shall see visions* (that is, divinely granted appearances)" (Acts 2:17). In the next pages I want to tell about a divinely granted appearance I had when I was a young man 33 years old.

At the time of this experience I was conducting a tent revival in Rockwall, Texas, during the latter part of August and the first part of September 1950. On Saturday, September 2, it rained all day—not a hard, driving rain, but a slow, gentle, soaking rain.

It was still raining that evening at church time, and when we arrived at the tent there were only about 40 people present.

Rockwall is in the blackland of northcentral Texas, and there is a saying that if you stick with the blackland when it is dry, it will stick with you when it is wet. Many of the people who had been attending the meetings lived in the country, and they couldn't get out to the service that night because of the rain and mud. That is why the crowd was small.

Because everyone present was a Christian, I gave a Bible lesson and then invited the people to come to the front to pray. It was about 9:30. (Let me say here that I no more expected what was to happen than I expected to be the first man to land on the moon. I hadn't been doing any unusual praying or fasting. I hadn't been praying that I would have such an experience. In fact, I hadn't even thought about such a thing.)

Everyone was praying around the front, and I knelt on the platform beside a folding chair near the pulpit. I began to pray in other tongues, and I heard a Voice say, "Come up hither." At first, I didn't realize that the Voice was speaking to me. I thought everybody heard it.

I See Jesus

"Come up hither," the voice said again. Then I looked and saw Jesus standing about where the top of the tent would be. As I looked up again, the tent had disappeared, the folding chairs had disappeared, every tent pole had disappeared, the pulpit had disappeared, and God permitted me to see into the spirit realm.

Jesus was standing there, and I stood in His Presence. He was holding a crown in His hands. This crown was so extraordinarily beautiful that human language cannot begin to describe it.

Jesus told me, "This is a soulwinner's crown. My people are so careless and indifferent. This crown is for every one of My children. I speak and say, 'Go speak to this one or pray for that one,' but my people are too busy. They put it off, and souls are lost because they will not obey Me."

When Jesus said that, I wept before Him. I knelt down and repented of my failures. Then Jesus said to me again, "Come up hither." It seemed as if I went with Him through the air until we came to a beautiful city. We did not actually go into the city, but we beheld it at close range as one might go up on a mountain and look down on a city in the valley. Its beauty was beyond words!

Jesus said that people selfishly say they are ready for Heaven. They talk about their mansions and the glories of Heaven while many around them live in darkness and hopelessness. Jesus said I should share my hope with them and invite them to come to Heaven with me.

Then Jesus turned to me and said, "Now let us go down to hell."

We came back down out of Heaven, and when we got to earth we didn't stop, but kept going. Numerous scriptures in the Bible refer to hell as being *beneath* us. For example, *"Hell from beneath is moved for thee to meet thee at thy coming . . . thou shalt be brought down to hell"* (Isa. 14:9,15). *"Therefore hell hath enlarged herself . . . and he . . . shall descend into it"* (Isa. 5:14).

We went down to hell, and as we went into that place I saw what appeared to be human beings wrapped in flames. I said, "Lord, this looks just like it did when I died and came to this place on April 22, 1933. You spoke and I came back up out of here. I then repented and prayed, seeking Your forgiveness, and You saved me. Only now I feel so different: I am neither afraid nor horrified, as I was then."

Jesus told me, "Warn men and women about this place," and I cried out with tears that I would.

He then brought me back to earth. I became aware that I was kneeling on the platform by the folding chair, and Jesus was standing by my side. As He stood there, He talked to me about my ministry. He told me some things in general that He later explained in more detail in another vision. Then Jesus disappeared and I realized I still was kneeling on the platform. I could hear people praying all around me.

The Angelic Messenger

About that time, the Holy Spirit came upon me again. It seemed as if a wind were blowing on me, and I fell flat on my face on the platform. As I lay under the power of God, it seemed as if I were standing high on a plain somewhere in space, and I could see for miles and miles around me, just as one can stand on the great plains of the United States and gaze off into the distance for miles.

I looked in every direction, but I couldn't see a sign of life anywhere. There were no trees or grass, no flowers or vegetation of any kind. There were no birds or animals. I felt so lonely. I was not conscious of my earthly surroundings.

As I looked to the west, I saw what appeared to be a tiny dot on the horizon. It was the only moving thing I could see. As I watched, it grew larger and came toward me, taking on shape and form.

Soon I could see it was a horse. As it came closer I could see a man upon the horse. He was riding toward me at full speed. As he approached, I could see he held the reins of the horse's bridle in his right hand, and in his left hand, high above his head, he held a scroll of paper.

When the horseman reached me, he pulled on the reins and stopped. I stood on his right. He passed the scroll from his left hand to his right hand and handed it to me.

As I unrolled the scroll, which was a roll of paper 12 or 14 inches long, he said, "Take and read." At the top of the page in big, bold, black print were the words "WAR AND DESTRUC-TION." I was struck dumb. He laid his right hand on my head and said, "Read, in the Name of Jesus Christ!"

I began to read what was written on the paper, and as the words instructed me, I looked and saw what I had just read about.

First I read about thousands upon thousands of men in uniform. Then I looked and *saw* these men marching, wave after wave of soldiers marching as to war. I looked in the direction they were going, and as far as I could see there were thousands of men marching.

I turned to read the scroll again, and then looked and saw what I had just read about. I saw many women—old women with snowy white hair, middle-aged women, young women, and teenagers. Some of the younger ones held babies in their arms. All of the women were bowed together in sorrow and were weeping profusely. Those who did not carry babies held their hands on their stomachs as they bowed over and wept. Tears flowed from their eyes like water.

I looked at the scroll again, and again I looked to see what I had read about. I saw the skyline of a large city. Looking closer, I saw the skyscrapers were burned-out hulls. Portions of the city lay in ruins. It was not written that just one city would be destroyed, burned, and in ruins, but that there would be many such cities destroyed.

America's Last Call

The scroll was written in the first person, and seemed as if Jesus Himself were speaking. I read, *"America is receiving her last call. Some nations already have received their last call and never will receive another."*

Then in larger print it said, "THE TIME OF THE END OF ALL THINGS IS AT HAND." This statement was repeated four or five times. Jesus also said this was the last great revival.

He went on to say, "All the gifts of the Spirit will be in operation in the Church in these last days, and the Church will do greater things than even the Early Church did. It will have greater power, signs, and wonders than were recorded in the Acts of the Apostles." He said that we have seen and experienced many healings, but we will now behold amazing miracles that have not been seen before.

Jesus continued, "More and more miracles will be performed in the last days which are just ahead, for it is time for the gift of the working of miracles to be more in prominence. We now have entered into the era of the miraculous.

"Many of My own people will not accept the moving of My Spirit, and will turn back and will not be ready to meet Me at my coming. Many will be deceived by false prophets and miracles of satanic origin. But follow the Word of God, the Spirit of God, and Me, and you will not be deceived. I am gathering My own together and am preparing them, for the time is short."

There were several other exhortations to watchfulness, to awaken and pray, and not to be deceived. Then I read, "As it was in the days of Noah, so also shall the coming of the Son of Man be. As I spoke to Noah and said, *'For yet seven days, and I will cause it to rain upon the earth forty days and forty nights; and every living substance that I have made will I destroy from off the face of the earth'* [Gen. 7:4], **so today I am speaking and giving America her last warning and call to repentance, and the time that is left is comparable to the last seven days of Noah's time."**

'Judgment Is Coming'

"Warn this generation, as did Noah his generation, for judgment is about to fall. And these sayings shall be fulfilled shortly, for I am coming soon." Jesus repeated, "This is the last revival. I am preparing My people for My coming. Judgment is coming, but I will call My people away, even unto Myself, before the worst shall come. But be thou faithful; watch and pray, for the time of the end of all things is at hand."

At the time I had this vision, naturally I interpreted the scenes to mean that America would experience the devastation of war. However, when I saw television and newspaper photographs of destruction wrought by student rebellion and race riots in the 1960s, I realized that these scenes partially fulfilled this vision. (This is why it is so important not to place your own interpretation on things God shows you.)

Those who were present that night under the tent said I read the scroll aloud for about 30 minutes. I cannot remember all of it. I handed the scroll back to the rider, and he rode away in the direction from which he had come.

Then I was conscious of the fact that I still lay flat on my face on the floor, and for a few minutes I remained there, feeling the glory of this miraculous visitation.

Again I heard a voice say, "Come up hither. Come up to the throne of God!"

The Throne of God

Again I saw Jesus standing about where the top of the tent should be, and I went to Him through the air. When I reached Him, together we continued on to Heaven. We came to the throne of God, and I beheld it in all its splendor. I was not able to look upon the face of God; I only beheld His form.

The first thing that attracted my attention was the rainbow about the throne. It was very beautiful. The second thing I noticed was the winged creatures on either side of the throne. They were peculiar-looking creatures and as I walked up with Jesus, these creatures stood with wings outstretched. They were saying something but they ceased and folded their wings. They had eyes of fire set all around their heads, and they looked in all directions at once.

I stood with Jesus in the midst, about 18 to 24 feet from the throne. I looked at the rainbow first, at the winged creatures, and then I started to look at the One who sat upon the throne.

Jesus told me not to look upon His face. I could only see a form of a Being seated upon the throne. Jesus talked with me for nearly an hour. I saw Him as plainly as I ever saw anyone in this life. I heard Him as He spoke to me.

Looking Into Love

And for the first time I actually looked into Jesus' eyes. Many times when relating this experience I am asked, "What did His eyes look like?" All I can say is that they looked like wells of living love. It seemed as if one could see half a mile deep into them, and the tender look of His love is indescribable. As I looked into His face and into His eyes, I fell at His feet.

I noticed then that His feet were bare, and I laid the palms of my hands on the top of His feet and laid my forehead on the backs of my hands. Weeping, I said, "O Lord, no one as unworthy as I should look upon your face!"

Jesus told me to stand upright on my feet. I stood up. He called me *worthy* to look upon His face, because He had called me and had cleansed me from all sin. He told me things concerning my ministry. He went on to say that He had called me before I was born. He said that although Satan had tried to destroy my life many times, His angels had watched over me and had cared for me.

Jesus told me that even as He had appeared to my mother before I was born and had told her, "Fear not, the child will be born," I would minister in the power of the Spirit and would fulfill the ministry He has called me to.

Then He talked to me about the last church I had pastored, saying that at that time, February 1949, I had entered into the first phase of my ministry. He said, "Some ministers I have called to the ministry live and die without getting into even the first phase of ministry I have for them." Jesus added that is one reason why many ministers die prematurely—they are living only in His permissive will!

God's Permissive Will

For 15 years I had been only in His permissive will. I had been a pastor for 12 years and had been in evangelistic work for three. During those years God permitted me to do it, but it wasn't His perfect will for my life. And He said I hadn't been waiting on *Him; He* had been waiting for *me* to obey Him.

Then He talked about the time I entered into the *first* phase of my ministry in 1949. He said I had been unfaithful and hadn't done what He had told me to do; I hadn't told the people what He had told me to tell them. I answered, "Lord, I wasn't unfaithful. I did obey You. I left my church and went out in the evangelistic field."

"Yes," He said, "you left the church and went out in evangelistic work. But you didn't do what I told you to do. The reason you didn't is because you doubted it was My Spirit who had spoken to you. You see, faith obeys My Word, whether it is the written Word of God or My Spirit who has spoken unto man."

I fell down before Him, saying, "Yes, Lord, I have failed and I am sorry." I repented with many tears because I had missed His will and had doubted His dealings with me.

"Stand up on your feet," He said. As I stood before Him again, He told me that I had entered into the *second* phase of my ministry in January 1950, and at that time He had spoken to me by prophecy and by the still small voice in my heart. In the next eight months, during this second phase of my ministry, I had believed, I had been faithful, and I had obeyed.

Now I was to enter into the *third* phase, He said. If I would be faithful to what He told me—if I would believe and obey Him—He would appear to me again. At that time I would enter into the *fourth* and final phase of my ministry.

Seeing Jesus' Wounds

Then the Lord said to me, "Stretch forth thine hand!" He held His own hands out before Him and I looked into them. For

some reason I expected to see a scar in each hand where the
nails had pierced His flesh. I should have known better, but
many times we get ideas that are not really scriptural, yet they
are accepted beliefs.

Instead of scars, I saw in the palms of His hands the wounds
of the crucifixion—three-cornered, jagged holes. Each hole was
large enough for me to have put my finger in it. I could see light
on the other side of the hole.

After the vision, I got out my Bible and turned to John chapter 20 to read about the time Christ appeared to His disciples
following His resurrection.

When Jesus first appeared to them, Thomas was not with
them. The disciples told Thomas they had seen the Lord, but
Thomas was unbelieving and said, *"Except I shall see in his
hands the print of the nails, and put my finger into the print of
the nails, and thrust my hand into his side, I will not believe"*
(John 20:25).

Eight days later while the disciples, including Thomas,
were together in a room, Jesus appeared again in their midst.
He turned to Thomas and said, *"Reach hither thy finger, and
behold my hands; and reach hither thy hand, and thrust it into
my side: and be not faithless, but believing."* Then Thomas,
knowing it was Jesus, exclaimed, *"My Lord and my God"*
(John 20:27,28).

I had deeper insight then into what Thomas had seen. He
could have put his finger into the wound in Jesus' hands,
and he could have thrust his hand into the wound in the
Lord's side.

As I looked upon the wounds in His hands outstretched
before me, I did as He instructed and held my hands out in
front of me. He laid the finger of His right hand in the palm of
my right hand and then in my left palm. The moment He
did, my hands began to burn as if a coal of fire had been
placed in them.

Jesus Gives Me a Special Anointing

Then Jesus told me to kneel down before Him. When I did, He laid His hand upon my head, saying that He had called me and had given me a special anointing to minister to the sick.

He went on to instruct me that when I would pray and lay hands on the sick, I was to lay one hand on each side of the body. If I felt the fire jump from hand to hand, an evil spirit or demon was present in that body causing affliction. I should call him out in Jesus' Name, and the demon or demons would have to go.

If the fire or the anointing in my hands did not jump from hand to hand, it was a case needing healing only. I should pray for the person in Jesus' Name, and if he would believe and accept it, the anointing would leave my hands and go into that person's body, driving out the disease and bringing healing. When the fire or anointing left my hands and went into the person's body, I would know he was healed.

I fell at Jesus' feet and pleaded, "Lord, don't send me. Send somebody else, Lord. *Please* don't send me. Just give me a little church to pastor somewhere. I would rather not go, Lord. I have heard so much criticism of those who pray for the sick. I just want a commonplace ministry."

Jesus rebuked me, saying, "I'll go with you and stand by your side as you pray for the sick, and many times you will see Me. Occasionally I will open the eyes of someone in the audience and they will say, 'Why, I saw Jesus standing by that man as he prayed for the sick.'"

Jesus asked me, "Who called you? Me or the people?"

"Well, You did, Lord."

'Don't Fear People'

He explained that I should fear Him and not people, because even though people may criticize me, they are not my judge. I will stand before His Judgment Seat one day to give an account to Him for what I have done with this ministry, whether I have used it rightly or wrongly.

"All right, Lord," I said. "I'll go if You'll go with me. I'll do my best and be as faithful as I know how to be."

Then there swelled up within my heart a love such as I had never known for those who criticize this type of ministry. I said, "Lord, I'll pray for them, for they don't know, or they wouldn't say the things they do. Lord, I've said similar things, but I didn't realize or see as I do now, and neither do they. Forgive them, Lord."

Then He said, "Go thy way, my son; fulfill thy ministry and be thou faithful, for the time is short."

As I walked away from the throne of God, Jesus told me, "Be sure to give Me all the praise and glory for all that is done, and be careful about money. Many of my servants whom I have anointed for this type of ministry have become money-minded and have lost the anointing and ministry I gave them.

"There are many who would pay much to be delivered. Many parents in the world have children whose little bodies are twisted, and they would give thousands of dollars for their healing. Many of them shall be delivered as you lay your hands on them, but you must not accept a charge for your ministry. Accept offerings as you have been doing. You must go your way. Be faithful, for the time is short."

Jesus then journeyed with me back to the earth, and I realized that I still lay on my face on the floor. He talked with me there a moment and then disappeared.

My hands burned for three days just like I had a coal of fire in each of them. Now when I wait upon the Lord in prayer and fasting, the same anointing comes upon me again.

I thank God I have seen polio-stricken children delivered and made well and straight, some of them walking immediately and others being healed gradually.

I have thought about this vision many times. Now more than four decades later, I am convinced we are nearer the end of time than ever before. We read in Second Peter 3:8 that *"one day is with the Lord as a thousand years, and a thousand years as one day."* Therefore, these years since the vision would be a very small fraction of time in God's sight.

As I stated earlier, I am convinced that a partial fulfillment of the burned-out cities I saw in the vision were the American cities that suffered so much looting and burning during the civil disobedience in the 1960s.

Judgment came, and judgment is yet to come. The only thing that can save America from the judgment of God is genuine repentance—a turning to God.

Modern Church to Do Exploits

In the vision, Jesus said that all the gifts of the Spirit would be in operation in the Church in these last days. He said that the modern Church would do greater exploits than the Acts of the Apostles records. I have seen this fulfilled in the years since the vision. In my own ministry I have seen healings as miraculous as any we read about in the Bible.

Acts 3 tells of the man lame from birth who sat daily at the gate of the Temple begging alms of those who entered. Peter said, *"Silver and gold have I none; but such as I have give I thee: In the name of Jesus Christ of Nazareth rise up and walk"* (Acts 3:6). The man was instantly healed. He leaped, walked, and praised God for his deliverance. We see in our ministry today cripples who are healed in the Name of Jesus.

On the Day of Pentecost, 120 people were baptized in the Holy Spirit. This was the largest number filled with the Holy Spirit at one time ever recorded in the Bible. But in my own meetings I have seen several hundred filled in one service; and in other meetings in which I have participated, as many as

500 have been baptized in the Holy Spirit, speaking with other tongues, within 15 minutes' time.

The Bible tells of instances in which as many as 3,000 or 5,000 turned to Christ in one day (Acts 2:41; 4:4). In these last days, however, we have reports of meetings in which tens of thousands of people are saved in one meeting.

For example, my longtime friend Dr. T.L. Osborn once preached in Calabar, Nigeria, to a crowd that government officials estimated was 500,000 persons. And Dr. Billy Graham preached at the largest Christian gathering in history in June 1973 in Seoul, South Korea. It is estimated that 1,100,000 attended that one service. A total of 3,210,000 attended the five-day Graham crusade and 72,365 decisions were recorded for the entire crusade.

So in these last days as we await Jesus' Coming, we are seeing as many great miracles around the world as we find recorded in the Acts of the Apostles!

In the vision in 1950, when Jesus told me about the special anointing He was giving me, He said, "If the anointing leaves you, fast and pray until it comes back." Now whenever the anointing wanes, I wait upon the Lord in prayer and fasting, and the same anointing comes upon me again.

However, I no longer lay one hand on each side of the person I am praying for to determine if an evil spirit is causing the affliction. Two years later the Lord gave me further instructions in a vision about dealing scripturally with the devil which I will discuss in detail in another chapter.

In the first vision, the Lord told me that He would appear to me again, and He has on several occasions. In the vision two years later, He said, "From this moment on, the gift that is known in my Word as the gift of discerning of spirits will operate in your ministry." With the operation of this gift, I can know when a person's body is oppressed by an evil spirit; therefore, this greater gift of the Holy Spirit is in manifestation as the Spirit wills.

Called From the Womb

Jesus told me in the first vision, "I called you before you were born. I separated you from your mother's womb." This was contrary to my beliefs at that time. However, looking into God's Word, I read where the Lord had said the same thing to Jeremiah concerning his ministry—the Lord had called him before he was born too (Jer. 1:5).

A week after this first vision, my mother visited me, and I related the vision to her. I told her that the Lord had said to me, "I called you before you were born. I separated you from your mother's womb. Satan tried to destroy your life before you were born and has tried many times since, but my angels have watched over you and have cared for you until this present hour.

"I appeared to your mother before you were born and told her to fear not; the child would be born and would bear witness concerning my Second Coming."

When Momma heard this, she almost jumped out of her chair. During the months before I was born, she had experienced many difficulties. My father was away much of the time, and she didn't know where he was. She didn't have adequate food to eat. Her parents lived fewer than three blocks away, but because they had opposed her marrying my father, she was reluctant to go home and ask them for help.

"I was just too proud to ask them for anything," she told me. "Not having enough food, I became ill, and for my baby's sake, I decided to swallow my pride and go to my parents and ask for something to eat. This was just a few days before you were born prematurely."

My Mother's Vision

My mother continued, "I started down the street, and when I got as far as the front of Aunt Mary's house, I heard a sound like wind blowing through the trees. I could hear tree leaves stirring, yet there was not a single tree anywhere nearby. I became frightened, and I looked up to the sky. It was a bright, sunny August day. Not a cloud dotted the pure blue sky.

"I walked on a few steps and heard the sound again like wind blowing through trees. I looked up again, and this time I saw one white cloud. At first it seemed to be hanging in the sky. Then it began to descend, and as it did, a form took shape upon it. Jesus came right down out of the sky and stood before me.

"Jesus said, 'Fear not. The child shall be born, for he shall bear witness concerning my Second Coming.' He was trying to tell me that my child would take part in the revival that would usher in the coming of the Son of Man. He would not be the only one, of course, but he would have a part in the last great move of God's Spirit.

"I became so frightened that I began to run, and I ran the rest of the way to my mother's house. When I arrived there, pale and out of breath, my mother asked, 'What is it? You look like you've just seen a ghost!' I immediately told her what I had just witnessed, but I never told anyone else. And she would never talk about it, either. We just weren't used to such things, and we were afraid people would think I had lost my mind."

As I listened to my mother tell of her experience before I was born, it fit right in with what the Lord had shown me in this vision.

Chapter 3

If—The Badge of Doubt

My second vision of Jesus occurred about a month after the first. I was conducting a revival meeting in the state of Oklahoma. I had told the congregation what the Lord had shown me about ministering to the sick and also about the anointing in my hands.

One night while I was ministering to the sick, a man in the healing line told me he had tuberculosis of the spine. He said he had been through three clinics and all the doctors had given him the same diagnosis: He was beyond medical help at that time. The man's spine was as stiff as a board.

In praying for him, I laid one hand on his chest and one hand on his back. When I did, the fire or anointing, jumped from hand to hand. I knew immediately that his body was oppressed by an evil spirit. I commanded the spirit, saying, "You foul spirit that oppresses this man's body, I command you to come out of his body in the Name of the Lord Jesus Christ!"

And then I made a terrible mistake: I got into unbelief. It is easy to get into unbelief sometimes, no matter who we are and not even realize it.

I said to the man, "See if you can stoop over and bend your back. Try to touch your toes." The word "if" is the badge of doubt. When I said, "See *if* you can," that was doubt. (God will put up with a certain amount of doubt in a young Christian who doesn't know any better, but when one is enlightened in God's Word, the Lord won't let him get by with it.)

The man tried to bend over, but he couldn't. His back was as stiff as ever. I laid my hands upon him again, one hand on his chest and one hand on his back, and I felt the fire jump from hand to hand. Again I commanded, "You foul spirit that oppresses this man's body, I command you to come out of him in the Name of the Lord Jesus Christ!"

Again I said to the man, "See *if* you can stoop over. Bend your back and touch your toes." His back was as immovable as before, because I was acting in unbelief and didn't realize it.

Then I said, "Well, we will try (which is unbelief, too) the third time." I laid one hand on his chest and the other on his back. Again I had the manifestation of the anointing in my hands.

For the third time I said, "You foul spirit that oppresses this man's body, I command you to come out of him in the Name of the Lord Jesus Christ!" To the man I said, "Now see *if* you can stoop over. See *if* you can bend down." He couldn't, of course.

I gave up and went on to pray for the next person. The man walked back down the aisle.

I was standing on the platform about three feet to the right of the pulpit. As the next person stepped up to be prayed for, I looked over to my left for some unknown reason, and I saw Jesus standing there as plainly as any man I had ever seen in my life! I thought everybody saw Him, but I learned later that no one in the congregation saw or heard Him except me. The congregation heard what I said, but they didn't see or hear anyone else.

Jesus was standing beside the pulpit. I could have reached out and touched Him. He pointed His finger at me and said, "I said that in My Name the demon or demons will leave!"

"Lord, I know You said that. It has been only a month since You appeared to me in Rockwall, Texas, and told me to command the demon or demons to come out in your Name. I told the demon to come out of that man, but he didn't."

Again Jesus pointed His finger at me and said, "I said, in My Name call out the demons and they *will* leave the body!"

"I know You said that, Lord, and I commanded the spirit to leave this man's body in the Name of the Lord Jesus Christ, but he didn't go."

Jesus put His finger in my face and said for the third time, *"I said in My Name the demons will go!* Call them out in My Name, and they will leave the body in My Name!"

Weakly, I replied again, "Lord, I know You said that. It happened just a month ago, and it is as fresh in my mind as if You said it last night. I know what You told me. And I did tell that demon to leave this man's body, but he didn't go."

I think I know how Jesus looked when He drove the money-changers out of the Temple, as recorded in Mark chapter 11. Suddenly it seemed as if His eyes shot fire; I could see flashes of lightning in them.

For the fourth time He jabbed His finger at me and said emphatically, *"Yes, but I said the demons will go!"* Then He disappeared.

I realized then that I had acted in unbelief. We sometimes think that if we have a special gift or anointing to minister, it always will work—but that is not the case. No matter how much authority we might have, no matter how many special gifts we might have, or how much power we might possess, they all work by faith and *faith only.*

When I realized I had exercised doubt instead of faith, I saw my mistake. I called the man to come back to the platform. He was standing at the rear of the auditorium and hadn't gone back to his seat yet.

I pointed to him and said, "Come back up here, Brother." He retraced his steps back up the aisle. I stood on the platform waiting for him to come around to the altar to where I was. The instant he stood before me, I slapped him on the back, and with my other hand on his chest I said, "Satan, I told you to leave this body! Out you go in the Name of the Lord Jesus Christ!" Then I said to the man, "Now, my brother (I didn't put an 'if' in it this time), stoop over and touch your toes!"

Instantly his back was limber. The tuberculosis of the spine was gone. The spine which had been as stiff as a board was healed. He could stoop over and touch his toes as well as any normal person. He was completely well!

Because this man had come to our meeting from Arkansas, we didn't see him until two weeks later. He came back to be in the last Saturday night service.

I asked him if he was still able to stoop over and touch his toes.

"Yes, I am still free," he said with a big smile lighting his face. He stepped out into the aisle, stooped over, touched the floor, and went through several exercises to prove that he was still limber and free.

This experience demonstrated to me once and for all the importance of following God's Word explicitly. God is no respecter of persons (Acts 10:34). And I learned that *no matter who we are, if we move in unbelief, we will stop the flow of God's power.*

Chapter 4

How Satan Influences Lives Today

My third vision of Jesus occurred in December 1952 in Broken Bow, Oklahoma, where I was conducting a meeting in a Full Gospel church. During my two-week stay there, I stayed in the parsonage with the pastor and his wife and their 11-year-old daughter.

One night after the service, we had returned to the parsonage and were having a sandwich and a glass of milk in the kitchen. As we talked about the things of the Lord, time slipped away from us.

The pastor's little girl was sitting there with us, and finally she became sleepy and said, "Daddy, it's getting late, and I have to get up early in the morning to go to school. Won't you come pray with me now?" It was their custom that he always prayed with her at night and then tucked her into bed.

The pastor looked at his watch and exclaimed, "It's 11:30! Why, I never dreamed it was that late. We have been sitting here talking for two hours." Then he said to his daughter, "Come here, honey. We'll just kneel down here and Brother Hagin can have prayer with us. Then you can go to bed."

As we knelt together in that kitchen, each of us beside a chair, I was in the Spirit before my knees ever touched the floor.

To some who might wonder what it means to be "in the Spirit," let me refer to what the Bible says about it.

When the Apostle John was on the isle of Patmos, the Bible says he *"was in the Spirit on the Lord's day, and heard behind me a great voice, as of a trumpet, Saying, I am Alpha and Omega, the first and the last: and, What thou seest, write in a book"* (Rev. 1:10,11).

The Lord Himself appeared to John, giving him a message to give to the seven churches in Asia Minor, and revealing to him things to come.

In Acts chapter 10, the Bible tells of the time when Peter was in the Spirit. Peter fell into a trance and saw a vision.

In this vision, the Lord told Peter to take the Gospel of salvation to the Gentiles. Until this time, the Gospel had been limited to the Jews.

Acts 10:10 says that Peter "fell into a trance." When this happens, a person's physical senses are *suspended.* This doesn't mean the person is unconscious or that he has fainted. It simply means that the physical senses are not operating at the moment the person is caught up into the Spirit. God permits him to see into the spirit realm or to see whatever He wants him to see.

Kneeling in a White Cloud

On this night in 1952 in the parsonage kitchen, my physical senses were suspended. At that moment I didn't know I was kneeling beside a kitchen chair. It seemed as if I was kneeling in a white cloud that enveloped me.

Immediately I saw Jesus. He seemed to be standing above me, about as high as the ceiling is from the floor. He began to talk to me. "I am going to teach you concerning the devil, demons, and demon possession," He began. "From this night forward, what is known in My Word as the gift of discerning of spirits will operate in your life when you are in the Spirit."

Before I go any further in relating this vision, let me explain something which I feel is very significant. Notice that Jesus said, "This will operate when you are in the Spirit." Many times we seem to think that *man* operates these gifts of the Spirit. However, man doesn't. They are manifested through him by the Holy Spirit: *"But the manifestation of the Spirit is given to every man to profit withal"* (1 Cor. 12:7). We do not have a thing in the world to do with the operation of the gifts other than the fact that they are manifested through us.

Jesus said to me, "When you are in the Spirit, discerning of spirits will operate." It won't operate at any particular time we might want it to operate. In other words, we cannot push a button and turn the gift on and off.

To illustrate, let me tell of two incidents that have happened in my ministry. The first happened the month following this vision. In January 1953, I was conducting a meeting in Tyler, Texas. I had been invited to stay with the pastor during the meeting, and I arrived at the parsonage the day before the meeting was to start.

After helping me with my luggage and showing me to my room, the pastor sat down to talk with me while I unpacked my suitcases. In the course of our conversation he said, "I trust that my niece will receive her healing while you are here." He went on to explain that she had cancer of the lungs. Because his brother, the girl's father, was not financially able to pay the girl's medical bills, the pastor had taken on the responsibility himself.

"I put her through one clinic and wasn't satisfied with their diagnosis," he said, "so I put her through another clinic. Both of them confirmed that as far as they could determine from all the tests, she has cancer of the left lung.

"The doctors insisted on operating immediately, saying, 'Even if we take out one lung, she could live. But she cannot live without any lungs.' When my niece said she would like to wait a week before undergoing surgery so she could fast and pray about it, the doctors said, 'It may be too late, for in a week's time it may spread too far.'

"Nevertheless, she insisted on a week's time to fast and pray. At the end of the week she decided not to have the operation. She said, 'I knew two women who had cancer of the lung. One was operated on, and the other wasn't. Both of them died. One lived just a couple years longer. What is two years? I will trust God to heal me and if He doesn't, if I die, I'll die!'"

Many weeks had now come and gone, and the girl was bedfast. The doctors said it was too late for an operation because the cancer had spread to both lungs. They were feeding her six times a day, but she was still losing weight. "We are planning to bring her to your services for prayer," the pastor said.

It was my custom then to hold special healing services each Tuesday and Friday night. On the first Tuesday night of the meeting, they got the girl out of bed and brought her to the service. I ministered to her by laying on of hands, but nothing happened. On Friday night they brought her again. I also prayed for her the Tuesday and Friday nights of the following week.

Four times I laid hands on her and nothing happened. I say this to point out that if I were exercising the gifts of the Spirit, I would already have healed her. But remember that Jesus said, "When you are *in the Spirit,* this gift of discerning of spirits will operate."

We continued the meeting into the third week, and on that Tuesday they brought her to church again. When she stood before me this time I was suddenly in the Spirit; suddenly the Spirit of God enveloped me like a cloud.

This young girl and I were standing in the midst of the white cloud. As I looked at her, I saw fastened to the outside of her body over her left lung (for this is where the cancer started), an evil spirit or imp. He looked very similar to a small monkey hanging onto her body, as a monkey would hang onto a tree limb.

God permitted me to see into the realm of the spirit to see this evil spirit. I addressed the spirit and said, "You foul spirit that is oppressing this girl's body, you have to leave." No one else in the congregation saw or heard anything but me, but they heard what I said.

The evil spirit replied, "I know I have to leave if you tell me to, but I don't want to."

"In the Name of the Lord Jesus Christ, I command you to leave this body!" I said. I watched as the evil spirit turned loose of the girl and fell to the floor. Then I said, "Not only must you leave this body, but you also must leave this building!" He ran down the aisle of the church and out the door.

The girl immediately lifted her hands and began praising God, saying, "I am free, I am free!" She had been a member of a Full Gospel church for 15 years—since she was a child of 8—and had been seeking the baptism of the Holy Spirit, but had never received it. In this instant, she received the Holy Spirit and began to speak with other tongues as the Spirit of God gave her utterance.

That same week she went back to her doctors and requested new X-rays and tests of her lungs. She still looked no better outwardly. She was frail and run-down. The doctors told her that more tests were not necessary; they had done everything they could for her. She insisted, however, so they began to make new X-rays and to run the usual tests.

"Something has happened!" the doctors exclaimed. They ran another set of tests and took more X-rays. Finally convinced, they said, "We cannot find any trace of cancer. It is all gone. Your lungs are clear. We wouldn't have believed it possible if we hadn't had the X-rays and tests to prove that you had had cancer. What happened to you?"

She explained exactly what had happened, that it was God's power that had made her completely whole. They said, "Well, all we can say is that we know the condition you were in and that you are now completely well. And if you like, we will sign an affidavit stating that you had cancer of the lungs, but now it is gone."

The point I am making is that if I had been the one doing the healing, I would have done so the first time I prayed for her rather than the fifth time. This is what Jesus meant when He said, "This gift of the Spirit will operate when you are in the Spirit."

A similar incident took place when I was conducting a meeting in 1958 in Pueblo, Colorado. While we were having special prayer for the sick one night, a man from Colorado Springs came forward. He told me that he was nervous, couldn't sleep, and was on tranquilizers. His wife later told me that they were about to commit him to a mental institution.

Seeing Demonic Oppression

I laid hands on him and prayed that his nerves would be healed and his body would be healed from the top of his head to the soles of his feet. Then I went on to pray for the next person in the healing line. I continued praying for others for about ten minutes more. This man had gone back to his seat, which was on my right. When I looked over at him, immediately I was in the Spirit. God permitted me to see into the spirit realm, and I saw an evil spirit sitting on this man's shoulder. The spirit's arms were around the man's head in an armlock. I could see this, but no one else in the congregation was aware of what was going on.

I called the man to come to me, and when he stood in front of me, I said, "You foul spirit that oppresses this man's mind, I command you to leave his body right now in the Name of

Jesus!" When I said that, the spirit turned loose of him and fell to the floor.

The evil spirit said to me, "I don't want to leave this man, but I know if you tell me to, I have to."

"Not only are you to leave this body, but you are to leave this building at once!" I commanded, and he ran out the side door.

A broad smile crossed the man's face. He threw his hands into the air and shouted, "I am free! I am free!" Although I hadn't mentioned what I had seen in the vision, the man said, "It seemed as if there was an iron band around my head and it was being screwed tighter and tighter. More and more pressure was being put on it. Suddenly it just popped off and was gone."

Do such healings last? Ten years later we heard from this man when he called our office in Tulsa for prayer for one of his children. He was still rejoicing in his freedom from demonic oppression.

These are just two of many examples I could give to illustrate the operation of the Spirit in my life, and how it is not something which we can control but which operates as God wills. There are no magic buttons we can push to operate spiritual gifts; it is only as the Lord leads.

Many suppose that the apostles carried these spiritual gifts around with them and operated them at will. But this certainly was not the case when Paul and Silas were at Philippi. They were there because God had led them into Macedonia by a vision. Lydia, a seller of purple dye, was saved as a result of their ministry.

Paul and Silas were in the city of Philippi for several days, and while there, *"It came to pass, as we went to prayer, a certain damsel possessed with a spirit of divination met us, which brought her masters much gain by soothsaying: The same followed Paul and us, and cried, saying, These men are the servants of the most high God, which shew unto us the way of salvation"* (Acts 16:16–17).

This girl had a spirit of divination, which is soothsaying or fortune-telling. She knew who Paul and Silas were by the evil spirit that was in her. In other words, that evil spirit knew them. The girl herself didn't know them because she had never seen them before, yet she said, *"These men are the servants of the most high God."*

Then we read, *"And this she did many days. But Paul, being grieved, turned and said to the spirit, I command thee in the name of Jesus Christ to come out of her. And he came out the same hour"* (Acts 16:18).

As the Spirit Wills

It is evident that Paul had the gift of discerning of spirits in operation in his ministry. Yet the Scripture says that the girl followed them around for many days. Why didn't Paul command the evil spirit to leave her on the first day? Why didn't he do it on the second day? The answer is simply that the gift didn't operate when Paul *wanted* it to operate, but when the Spirit willed for it to operate. Until he had the operation of the Spirit, Paul was just as helpless as any other person to deal with the situation!

We need to understand the Scriptures concerning this in order to be open to God and to look to Him in prayer for the manifestation of spiritual gifts.

Getting back to the 1952 vision God gave me late that night in Broken Bow, Oklahoma, the Lord said to me, "From this night forward, what is known in my Word as the gift of discerning of spirits will operate in your life when you are in the Spirit. I will show you how these spirits get ahold of people and dominate them—even Christians, if they allow them to."

Jesus went on to say, "There are four classes of demons or evil spirits." He said that they are divided into four groups as mentioned in Ephesians: *"For we wrestle not against flesh and blood, but against* **principalities,** *against* **powers,** *against the* **rulers of the darkness of this world,** *against* **spiritual wickedness** [wicked spirits] *in high places"* (Eph. 6:12).

The Lord said, "There are four divisions: (1) principalities, (2) powers, (3) rulers of the darkness of this world, (4) and wicked spirits in high places or in the heavenlies. The highest spirits with which you have to deal are the rulers of the darkness of this world."

He went on talking to me about the fact that the Word of God says that the whole world lies in darkness, but we who are believers are children of light and not of darkness. He referred to a number of Scriptures, including the following:

"Be ye not unequally yoked together with unbelievers: for what fellowship hath righteousness with unrighteousness? and what communion hath light with darkness?" (2 Cor. 6:14). Believers are called light, and unbelievers are called darkness.

Colossians chapter 2 tells of Christ's death on the Cross and resurrection from the dead: *"And having spoiled principalities and powers, he made a shew of them openly, triumphing over them in it"* (v. 15). In other words, Christ, in His death, burial, and resurrection, spoiled or defeated these same principalities and powers that we must deal with.

Rulers of the Unsaved

The Lord went on to say, "The highest types of demons with which you have to deal on earth—the rulers of the darkness of this world—rule all unsaved people, that is, all those who are in darkness. They rule over them and dominate them.

"That is why people do and say things they don't intend to. That is why some good people say, 'I would never do anything like that,' and before a year has passed they have done something worse. This is because they are dominated by the rulers of the darkness of this world. They are in the kingdom of darkness.

And whether you want to admit it or not, even your close friends and relatives or whoever it may be, if they are unsaved, are dominated by these spirits who are rulers of the darkness of this world.

"It is always one of these rulers of the darkness of this world that possesses a person. They rule not only those who are within the darkness of this world, but they also tell the powers what to do. Then the powers rule over the principalities and tell them what to do. The lowest type of demons have very little to do. They do very little thinking of their own and are told what to do.

"Now I will show you how these evil spirits get ahold of people when they are allowed to," the Lord said to me. Suddenly in the vision I saw a woman. I immediately recognized her as being the former wife of a minister. I had been introduced to her and her husband on one occasion. Other than that, I didn't know either of them and I had no communication with either of them in any way. I only knew that she had since left her husband.

"This woman was a child of Mine," the Lord said. "She was in the ministry with her husband. She was filled with the Spirit, and the gifts of the Spirit were operating in her life. One day an evil spirit came to her and whispered in her ear, 'You are a beautiful woman. You could have had fame, popularity, and wealth, but you have been cheated in life by following in the Christian walk.' The woman realized that this was an evil spirit and she said, 'Get thee behind me, Satan.' The spirit left her for a period.

"By and by the same evil spirit returned. He sat on her shoulder and whispered in her ear, 'You are a beautiful woman, but you have been robbed by taking this lowly walk of Christianity and living a separated life.' Again she recognized this as Satan and said, 'Satan, I resist you in the Name of Jesus,' and he left her for a while.

"But he came back again and sat on her shoulder, whispering the same things in her ear. This time she began to entertain these thoughts, for she liked to think she was beautiful. As she began to think along the lines the devil suggested to her, she became obsessed with that thinking."

Then in the vision I saw the woman become as transparent as glass, and I saw a black dot in her mind. "That dot represents the fact that she is obsessed in her thinking with this evil spirit," the Lord said. "At first she was oppressed on the outside, but as she allowed the devil's suggestion to take ahold of her thoughts, her mind became obsessed. She wanted to think, 'I am a beautiful woman. I could have wealth and popularity, but I have been robbed in life.' Still, it wasn't too late. She could have resisted; she could have refused to think those thoughts. Then the evil spirit would have fled from her, and she would have remained free. But she *chose* otherwise.

"Finally she left her husband and went out into the world, seeking the fame and wealth which the devil offered. She took up with one man after another. After a time that thing got down into her spirit." In the vision I saw the black dot move from her head to her heart, and then the woman said, "I don't want the Lord anymore. Just leave me alone."

I said, "Lord, why are You showing this to me? Do You want me to pray for this woman? Do You want me to cast the devil out of her?"

"No, I don't want you to pray and cast the devil out of her," the Lord answered, "because you couldn't anyway. She wants that evil spirit, and as long as she wants it, she can have it."

"Then why did You show this to me, Lord?"

"I have shown this to you for two reasons: first, so you could see how an evil spirit will get ahold of a person, even a child of God, if they will let him. Second, I want you to deal with the evil spirit that is operating through that woman and harassing and intimidating the ministry of her former husband."

"How do I do that?" I asked. The minister was in the same state I was in, but the woman was in another state.

"There is no distance in the realm of the spirit," the Lord said. "Simply speak to that spirit and command him, in My Name, saying, 'You foul spirit that is operating in the life of this woman [calling her name], that is harassing and embarrassing the ministry of the servant of the Lord [calling her husband's name], I command you to desist in your operations and stop in your maneuvers this moment."

In the Spirit I said those words, and immediately that spirit ceased to operate through her to intimidate that minister. From that day forward the minister was never again troubled by her or that spirit.

"Lord, what will happen to her?" I asked.

"She will spend eternity in the regions of the damned, where there is weeping and gnashing of teeth," He answered. And in the vision I saw her go down into the pit of hell. I heard her awful screams.

"This woman was Your child, Lord. She was filled with Your Spirit and had part in the ministry. Yet You said not to pray for her. I cannot understand this!"

The Lord reminded me of the following Scripture: *"If any man see his brother sin a sin which is not unto death, he shall ask, and he shall give him life for them that sin not unto death. There is a sin unto death: I do not say that he shall pray for it"* (1 John 5:16).

I said, "But, Lord, I always believed that the sin referred to in this Scripture is physical death, and that the person is saved although he has sinned."

"But that Scripture doesn't say physical death," the Lord pointed out. "You are adding something to it. If you will read the entire fifth chapter of First John, you will see that it is talking about life and death—spiritual life and spiritual death—and this is spiritual death. This refers to a believer who can sin a sin unto death, and therefore I say that you shall not pray for it. I told you not to pray for this woman because she sinned a sin unto death."

"This really disrupts my theology, Lord. Would you explain some more?" I asked. (Sometimes we need our theology disrupted if it is not in line with the Word.)

Jesus reminded me of the following Scripture:

HEBREWS 6:4–6

4   For it is impossible for those who were once enlightened, and have tasted of the heavenly gift, and were made partakers of the Holy Ghost,

5   And have tasted the good word of God, and the powers of the world to come,

6   If they shall fall away, to renew them again unto repentance; seeing they crucify to themselves the Son of God afresh, and put him to an open shame.

"Yes, I know that Scripture, but my denomination said that 'those who were once enlightened' does not refer to Christians— it means lost persons who get under conviction."

The Lord said, "Remember, I told you this woman was My child. She was filled with the Holy Spirit, and she had part in the ministry. You will notice that the Scripture says, *'It is impossible for those who were once enlightened, and have tasted of the heavenly gift. . . .'* I am the Heavenly Gift. A man under conviction is enlightened, but he has not tasted of Me.

"The Word of God says, 'For God so loved the world, that he gave his only begotten Son, that whosoever believeth in him should not perish, but have everlasting life' (John 3:16). I am the Heavenly Gift, and the man under conviction has not tasted of the Heavenly Gift. He sees his lost condition and he sees that he can be saved: *'For the wages of sin is death; but the gift of God is eternal life through Jesus Christ our Lord'* (Rom. 6:23). No one has *tasted* the heavenly gift, the gift of God, until he has received eternal life by *accepting* Me as Lord and Savior.

"Notice the words in this Scripture *'and were made partak-ers of the Holy Ghost* [this woman had been baptized in the Holy Spirit], *And have tasted the good word of God'* (Heb. 6:4–5); or as the *Phillips* translation reads, *'. . . who have known the wholesome nourishment of the Word of God.'*

"In other words, *baby Christians cannot commit the sin unto death.* It is to be regretted that baby Christians live as they sometimes do, and they say and do some things they should not. But I do not hold these things against them any more than you would hold things a little child may do against him, because he doesn't know any better.

"The person referred to in this Scripture—and that includes the woman I am showing you—has tasted the good Word of God; that is, he or she has grown beyond the baby Christian stage of Christianity. One Scripture says, *'As newborn babes, desire the sincere milk of the word, that ye may grow thereby'* (1 Peter 2:2). This woman had grown beyond the sincere milk of the Word. She had tasted the solid meat of the Word. She already had tasted of the 'powers of the world to come.' That means she had the gifts of the Spirit in operation in her life."

Jesus continued, "For one to commit 'a sin unto death,' he would need to have all five of these experiences:

1. Be enlightened (or convicted) to see his lost state, and to know that there is no way for him to be saved except through Jesus Christ.

2. Taste of the Heavenly Gift, which is Jesus.

3. Become a partaker of the Holy Spirit or be filled with the Holy Spirit.

4. Grow enough out of the babyhood stage to have tasted the good Word of God.

5. Have the powers of the world to come—the gifts of the Spirit—operating in his life.

"This woman had all these qualifications," Jesus said. *"And my Word says it is impossible 'If they shall fall away, to renew them again unto repentance; seeing they crucify to them-selves the Son of God afresh, and put him to an open shame'"* (Heb. 6:6).

I asked the Lord, "What sin is this, then?"

The Lord referred me to the following Scripture:

HEBREWS 10:26–29

26 For if we sin wilfully after that we have received the knowledge of the truth, there remaineth no more sacrifice for sins,

27 But a certain fearful looking for of judgment and fiery indignation, which shall devour the adversaries.

28 He that despised Moses' law died without mercy under two or three witnesses:

29 Of how much sorer punishment, suppose ye, shall he be thought worthy, who hath trodden under foot the Son of God, and hath counted the blood of the covenant, wherewith he was sanctified, an unholy thing, and hath done despite unto the Spirit of grace?

The Lord said to me, "The sin that this Scripture speaks about is that of the believer who turns his back upon Me. Notice the words in this Scripture, *'He that despised Moses' law died without mercy . . . Of how much sorer punishment, suppose ye, shall he be thought worthy, who hath trodden under foot the Son of God.'*

"Because of great persecution, the Hebrew Christians referred to in this passage were tempted to go back to Judaism, but if they went back, they would have trodden underfoot the Son of God. They would have counted the blood of the covenant an unholy thing, for they would be saying that Jesus is not the Messiah; He is not the Son of God. They turned their backs on Me. This is why Paul warned them that if they did that, it would be impossible to renew them unto repentance.

Forgiveness for Adultery

"It is sad that this woman left her husband for another man, but adultery is not the unpardonable sin. If she had turned back to Me in repentance, even though she might have had a hundred men, I would have forgiven her. Whatever she might have done, if she had asked Me to forgive her, I would have.

"Even if she had been a baby Christian when she said, 'I don't want Jesus anymore; leave me alone,' and didn't actually realize what she was doing, I would have forgiven her. If she had done that because she was tempted and pressed into it beyond measure, I would have forgiven her. *But she knew exactly what she was doing, and she acted willfully* when she said, 'I don't want Him anymore.' Therefore, I tell you not to pray for her. I merely showed you this so you might see how the devil can get ahold of Christians if they will permit him to."

Then in the vision I saw a man. I didn't recognize him. Jesus said, "I will show you another example of how demons get hold of a person and how to deal with them and cast them out."

I saw a evil spirit come and sit on the man's shoulder and whisper in his ear. This man was not a Christian, he was not born again. The man entertained the thoughts Satan gave him. Then I saw this evil spirit go into the man's mind.

Jesus said, "This evil spirit is one of the higher rulers of their world. They are the ones that get ahold of a man and eventually possess him. There are degrees of possession, and these spirits will bring other evil spirits with them."

Then the Lord reminded me of the passage in Mark's Gospel which tells the story of the maniac of Gadara.

MARK 5:2–7

2 And when he was come out of the ship, immediately there met him out of the tombs a man with an unclean spirit [notice here that the man had just one unclean spirit],

3 Who had his dwelling among the tombs; and no man could bind him, no, not with chains:

4 Because that he had been often bound with fetters and chains, and the chains had been plucked asunder by him, and the fetters broken in pieces: neither could any man tame him.

5 And always, night and day, he was in the mountains, and in the tombs, crying, and cutting himself with stones.

6 But when he saw Jesus afar off, he ran and worshipped him,

7 And cried with a loud voice, and said, What have I to do with thee, Jesus, thou Son of the most high God? I adjure thee by God, that thou torment me not.

Notice that the evil spirit knew Jesus. When Jesus asked him his name, he replied, *"My name is Legion: for we are many"* (v. 9). When Jesus cast the demons out they entered a herd of swine nearby, *"and the herd ran violently down a steep place into the sea, (they were about two thousand;) and were choked in the sea"* (v. 13).

Although only one evil *spirit possessed* this man from Gadara, as many as 2,000 were cast out and plunged headlong into the sea after entering the herd of swine!

In the vision, the evil spirit got ahold of the man and seemed to open his head like a trap door. Then I saw other spirits come and enter the man. Jesus said to me, "From now on when you come into the presence of anyone who is fully possessed with the devil, he will recognize you, just as the man you read about in Mark 5 recognized Me when he came into My Presence. Now walk up to this man, and when you do, the evil spirit will recognize you."

In the vision I walked up to the man, and immediately the demon that possessed him called out, "I know you."

I said, "Yes, I realize you know who I am, and I command you to be quiet right now in the Name of Jesus!"

The Lord went on to say, "These spirits will know you. Through the gift of discerning of spirits you will know what kind of spirit it is. You remember that in dealing with the man from Gadara I said, *'Come out of the man, thou unclean spirit.'* I discerned it was an unclean spirit, and I commanded him to come out."

In the case of this unsaved man in the vision who had the evil spirit, I knew immediately what kind of spirit possessed him, and I commanded that spirit to come out of him, but he didn't.

Jesus said, "To cast them out you sometimes have to know not only the kind of spirit they are but also their name or number. Notice in dealing with the man from Gadara, I said, *'Come out of the man, thou unclean spirit,'* but he didn't come out."

This was something I had completely overlooked, but on rereading Mark 5 I noticed it was true: *"And he* [Jesus] *asked him, What is thy name? And he answered, saying, My name is Legion: for we are many"* (v. 9)

Jesus brought something else to my attention concerning this passage. "If you had been present," Jesus said, "you would have heard what the evil spirit said, because he used the man's voice—the evil spirit talked through the man. When I asked what his name was, he replied, 'My name is Legion, for we are many.' Then he begged, 'Don't send us away out of the country.' That was the first unclean spirit that possessed the man's body who was doing the speaking—he used the man's voice.

"Then you will see in Mark 5:12, 'And all the devils besought him, saying, Send us into the swine, that we may enter into them.' All of the demons cried out at once. Had you been present at this time, you wouldn't have known what they were saying, unless you had the gift of discerning of spirits to see and hear in the spirit realm.

"I could hear all these evil spirits cry out because the gift of discerning of spirits was operating in my ministry. All of the demons besought Me—all of them spoke at once. They weren't talking out loud; that is, they weren't talking as a man would speak. They were speaking in the spirit realm."

I then walked up to the man in the vision. I discerned the kind of spirit that possessed him and commanded him to come out. Nothing happened. Jesus then said to ask his number, so I said, "How many of you are in this man?"

He said, "Nineteen more besides me."

I spoke to them, saying, "I command you and all 19 others to come out," and they came out. Then I asked the Lord, "Where do demons go when they come out?"

"They walk the dry places seeking rest, and they find none," He replied. Then I remembered the following Scripture:

MATTHEW 12:43–45

43 When the unclean spirit is gone out of a man, he walketh through dry places, seeking rest, and findeth none.

44 Then he saith, I will return into my house from whence I came out; and when he is come, he findeth it empty, swept, and garnished.

45 Then goeth he, and taketh with himself seven other spirits more wicked than himself, and they enter in and dwell there: and the last state of that man is worse than the first.

I asked the Lord, "Why can't we cast them into the pit and banish them from the earth forever?"

He said, "The time for this hasn't come yet. If it would have been possible to do that, when I was on earth, I would have cast them all into the pit. But you will remember on one occasion the demons cried out to Me, saying, *'What have we to do with thee, Jesus, thou Son of God ? art thou come hither to torment us before the time?'* (Matt. 8:29). You see, their time hasn't come yet. The time is coming when Satan and all his demons will be cast in the lake of fire where they will be forever."

While Jesus was talking to me, an evil spirit that looked like a monkey ran between Jesus and me and spread out something that looked like a black cloud or a smoke screen. I couldn't see Jesus anymore.

Then the demon began jumping up and down, waving his arms and legs, and yelling in a shrill voice, "Yakety-yak, yakety-yak, yakety-yak."

I paused for a moment. I could hear the voice of Jesus as He continued to talk to me, but I could not understand the words He was saying.

I thought to myself, *Doesn't the Lord know I am missing what He is saying? I need to get that—it is important—but I am missing it.* I wondered why Jesus didn't command the evil spirit to stop talking. I waited for a few more moments. Jesus continued talking as if He didn't even know the evil spirit were present. I wondered why the Lord didn't cast him out, but He didn't.

Finally, in desperation, I pointed my finger at the evil spirit and said, "I command you to be quiet in the Name of Jesus Christ!" He stopped immediately and fell to the floor. The black smoke screen disappeared and I could see Jesus once again. The spirit lay on the floor whimpering and whining like a whipped pup. I said, "Not only must you be quiet, but get up and get out of here!" He got up and ran away.

I was still wondering why Jesus had not stopped this evil spirit from interfering, and of course Jesus knew what I was thinking. He said, "If you hadn't done something about that, I couldn't have."

"Lord, I know I misunderstood You! You said You *couldn't* do anything about it, but You really meant that *You wouldn't.*"

"No," He said, "if you hadn't done something about that spirit, I couldn't have."

"But, Lord, You can do *anything.* To say You couldn't is different from anything I've ever heard preached or preached myself. That really upends my theology."

"Sometimes your theology needs upending," the Lord answered.

I said, "Lord, even though I am seeing You with my own eyes, even though I hear your voice speaking to me as plainly as any voice I have ever heard, I cannot accept that unless You prove it to me by the Word of God. For the Word says, *'In the mouth of two or three witnesses shall every word be established'* (2 Cor. 13:1). I will not accept any vision, I will not accept any revelation, if it cannot be proved by the Bible."

Instead of becoming angry with me for saying this, Jesus smiled sweetly and said, "I will give you not just two or three witnesses; I will give you four witnesses."

I said, "I have read through the New Testament 150 times and many portions of it more than that. If that is in there, I don't know about it."

"Son, there is a lot in there you don't know," the Lord pointed out. "There is not a single place in the New Testament where believers are ever told to pray against the devil and I will do anything about him. There is not one instance in any of the epistles written to the churches that said to tell God to rebuke the devil or do something about the devil. To pray that God the Father or I the Lord Jesus Christ will rebuke the devil or do anything about the devil, is a waste of time. God has done all He is going to do about the devil for the time being until the angel comes down from Heaven, takes the chain and binds him, and puts him into the bottomless pit.

"Every writer of the New Testament in writing to the Church always told *the believer* to do something about the devil. The believer has to have authority over the devil, or the Bible wouldn't tell him to do something about the devil:

MATTHEW 28:18–20

18 All power [or authority] is given unto me in heaven and in earth.

19 Go ye therefore, and teach all nations, baptizing them in the name of the Father, and of the Son, and of the Holy Ghost:

20 Teaching them to observe all things whatsoever I have commanded you: and, lo, I am with you alway, even unto the end of the world.

"You might say, 'But you could have done something about that evil spirit because this Scripture says you have all power

and authority in Heaven and in earth.' However, I have delegated my authority on the earth to the Church:

MARK 16:15–18

15 Go ye into all the world, and preach the gospel to every
creature.

16 He that believeth and is baptized shall be saved; but he
that believeth not shall be damned.

17 And these signs shall follow them that believe; In my
name shall they cast out devils; they shall speak with new
tongues;

18 They shall take up serpents; and if they drink any
deadly thing, it shall not hurt them; they shall lay hands on
the sick, and they shall recover.

"One of the first signs mentioned that will follow believers is that they should cast out devils. That means that in My
Name they will exercise authority over the devil. I delegated
My authority over the devil to the Church, and I can work only
through the Church, for I am the Head of the Church.

"In writing to believers, James said, *'Resist the devil, and he
will flee from you'* (James 4:7). James didn't say to get God to
resist the devil for you. He said, 'You resist the devil and he will
flee from *you.*'"

I looked up the word "flee" in the dictionary later and saw
that one definition is *to run from as in terror*. As I read that,
I remembered how the evil spirits in the vision had fled when
I had rebuked them. And since then I have seen them quake
and quiver in fear as I exercised my God-given authority over
them. They were not afraid of me, but rather of Jesus, whom I
represent.

Jesus continued, "Peter said, *'Be sober, be vigilant; because
your adversary the devil, as a roaring lion, walketh about, seeking whom he may devour'* (1 Peter 5:8). What are you going to
do: Throw up your hands and say, 'I am whipped'? No, a thousand times no! We read in First Peter 5:9, *'Whom resist stedfast*

in the faith.' You couldn't resist the devil if you didn't have authority over him. But you *do* have authority over him, and that is why you can resist him.

"Paul said in his writings to the Church at Ephesus, *'Neither give place to the devil'* (Eph. 4:27). This means you are not to give the devil any place in you. He cannot *take* any place unless you give him *permission* to do so. And you would have to have authority over him or this wouldn't be true!"

Then Jesus said to me, "Here are your four witnesses: I am the first, James is the second, Peter is the third, and Paul is the fourth. These are the four witnesses I told you I would give instead of just two or three. This establishes the fact that the believer has authority on earth, for I have delegated my authority over the devil to you on the earth. If you don't do anything about rebuking the devil, then nothing will be done, and that is why many times nothing *is* done."

Then I said, "Lord, You have told me about only three categories of evil spirits: the rulers of the darkness of this world, the powers, and the principalities. What about the wicked spirits in the heavenlies?"

He said, "You take care of the ones on earth. I will take care of those in the heavenlies."

Jesus exhorted me to be faithful, saying, "Fulfill your ministry. Be faithful, for the time is short." Then He disappeared.

I realized that I was still on my knees in the kitchen of that parsonage, and about an hour and a half had passed while I was caught up in this vision.

Chapter 5

I Have Come
to Answer Your Prayer

It was nearly five years later in 1957, when the Lord appeared to me again in my fourth vision of Him.

My wife and I had just returned to our home in Garland, Texas, after spending 16 months in meetings in California. We then held a meeting for our home Full Gospel church in Garland. It was during the third week of this meeting that I had another supernatural visitation from the Lord.

At the close of my message one night, a spirit of prayer descended upon the congregation and we all gathered around the altar to pray. We prayed for quite some time

After a while I got off my knees and sat on the steps to the platform. I was sitting there with my eyes open, singing in other tongues as the Spirit gave utterance, when suddenly I saw Jesus standing about three feet in front of me. He said, "I have come to answer your prayer."

I knew exactly what He was talking about. I had been praying for some time for my wife, who had a goiter. It was growing larger and larger until now she was having choking spells.

From the time we were first married, I had sensed in my spirit that Oretha would die at an early age, and I thought that perhaps this time was approaching. I prayed the rest of the night about this and said to the Lord, "I have obeyed You and have done Your will. I have left my church and my family and have been in the evangelistic field for many years. My wife has stayed at home and has been faithful to raise our children. I am still a young man (at that time I was in my 30s), and we have been married for many years. Please let me keep my wife."

In the vision the Lord said to me, "I have come to answer that prayer. Tell your wife to be operated on, for she will live and not die."

Although I didn't mention it to my wife, I had felt all along that if she were operated on she would die. She later told me that she had known for several years that she would die when she was operated on for this goiter.

But the Lord said to me, "She will live and not die. According to the natural course of events without divine intervention, she would die But I have heard your prayers and have come to answer them. She shall live . . ."

Then Jesus said something that absolutely melted me, and I have never been able to forget it. It blessed and helped me then, and it still blesses me.

He said, "I did this, son, just because you asked Me to. You don't know how I long to do for my children if they would only ask Me and believe Me. Many times they beg and cry and pray, but they don't believe. And I cannot answer their prayers unless they have faith, because I cannot violate my Word. But how often I long to help them if only they would let Me by taking Me at My Word and bringing Me their problems, trusting Me to undertake for them."

Again He said, "Tell your wife to be operated on, for she will live and not die." With those words He disappeared.

Even though the doctors were greatly concerned about my wife's condition, Oretha and I had great joy through it all because we knew the outcome in advance.

Chapter 6

The Angel's Visit

My fifth vision occurred in 1958 in Port Neches, Texas, while I was holding a revival meeting. One night as we were praying around the altar, a great spirit of prayer seemed to come upon the whole church. We prayed together for quite some time, and then I got up and sat in a chair on the platform.

I was sitting there with my eyes open, singing in other tongues, when the Lord Jesus suddenly appeared on the platform—and about three feet behind him stood a huge angel!

Jesus said to me, "I sent my angel to speak to you nearly a year ago out in California." I remembered the occasion, and I remembered that I had not responded to him.

That afternoon I had been lying across the bed in my house trailer meditating and reading my Bible, getting ready for the evening service. Suddenly I had the feeling that someone had come into the trailer. I looked, but I couldn't see anyone. But I was positive that someone had come through the door. It even seemed as if I had heard the door open and close. I sensed that someone was standing beside the bed. I reached out my hand to feel whatever might be there and said, "I know you are there. Who are you?"

There was no response. Although I never saw anyone, I sensed that someone stood there for a few moments, turned around, retraced his steps around the foot of the bed, and went back through the trailer and out the door.

Then I seemed to be led of the Spirit to open my Bible and read about the ministry of angels. I felt that an angel had come to me, but I had not yielded to the Holy Spirit nor opened my heart to the visitation.

We continued our ministry in the state of California. The children were traveling with us at that time, doing their school-work through correspondence courses, which we helped them with. They had been with us for about a year, and we decided that it was just too hard on them. They were doing a great deal of traveling, were in two services a day, and were trying to keep up with their studies. Therefore, we decided to return to our home in Garland so they could attend the public schools.

The people who had been renting our house moved out so we could move back, but we had sold all our furniture when we bought the house trailer, so we had to buy a whole houseful of new furniture. Of course, we had to go in debt to do so. This made our monthly payments extremely high, because we still were making payments on the trailer house, and car—not to mention our living expenses.

For more than a year we lacked about $100 every month in getting enough money to meet our budget. Therefore, we had to go in debt that much: I had to borrow $100 each month just to pay expenses and keep operating.

Back in 1956 the Lord had spoken to me, warning me that a recession was coming—not a depression, but a recession—and that I should prepare for it. The recession did come in 1957. Fifteen months later when the Lord appeared to me in the vision in Port Neches, I was still bearing the consequences of not having gotten ready for the recession.

The Lord said to me, "I sent my angel to warn you again when you were out in California, because I saw that you hadn't listened to the leading of my Spirit and hadn't responded to the warning. If you had yielded to the Holy Spirit (we can't see angels with the natural eye unless God so wills, for they are spirits), you would have been able to see into the realm of the spirit. By the discerning of spirits, you would have seen the angel, and he would have delivered his message to you. If you had received it, you would have been spared all this financial trouble."

When Jesus appeared to me 15 months had passed since the angel came to warn me about the recession, and I was going into debt each month for $100, my debt now totaled $1,500.

The Lord continued, "I am going to help you, however, with your finances."

We had been trying to sell our house trailer, but because the new ten-foot-wide models had just come on the market, it seemed no one wanted to buy our eight-foot-wide trailer.

Jesus continued, "Your house trailer will sell. But because you didn't listen when I told you to prepare for the coming recession, you'll have to bear the consequences of your disobedience for a while. Your house trailer will sell in seven months."

And He did help me. Although I had to make payments on the house trailer for seven more months because of my disobedience, the trailer was sold just as Jesus had said.

Jesus also said to me, "I am going to help you in your ministry as well," and He talked to me further about my ministry, admonishing me to be faithful. Then pointing to the angel standing beside Him, he said, "This is your angel."

"My angel?" I said.

"Yes, your angel. And if you will yield to the Holy Spirit, the gift of discerning of spirits will begin to operate, and you will see into the spirit realm. You will see your angel at times, but only as I will it. And he will give you guidance and direction concerning the things of life, for angels are ministering spirits who are sent to minister for those who are the heirs of salvation" (Heb. 1:14).

Everything that the Lord showed me in this vision concerning my finances and my ministry came to pass just as the Lord said it would.

Chapter 7

A Hospital Visitor

The sixth time the Lord appeared to me was in February 1959, while I was holding a revival meeting in El Paso, Texas.

I slipped and fell on my right elbow, hurting my arm rather severely. At first I thought it was broken, and because this was about 9:30 at night, I went to the hospital to have a doctor look at it and set the bones, if necessary.

About a block from the hospital, the Lord spoke to me and told me my arm was not broken; I had a fracture and had knocked my elbow out of place. The Lord also said this was the devil's work, but He would make it turn out for His glory and my good. He also told me He would talk to me about it later, and I should not fear or worry about anything.

At the hospital the doctor X-rayed my arm and confirmed what I already knew to be true. He explained that my elbow was knocked out of place and some chips were broken off the bone. This, he explained, was even worse than a broken arm, because the ligaments and muscles that hold the elbow in place would have to be put back in place. He said they would have to give me anesthetic to do this; otherwise, I would not be able to stand the pain.

Then, he said, I would have to be in the hospital for several days. After that I would have to wear a cast on my arm for at least four weeks, and then I would have to carry the arm in a sling for a while.

The next afternoon I was propped up in bed in my hospital room. I was fully dressed as I sat there, because I had been walking up and down the hospital corridors. I had sat in the lobby for a while before my dinner tray was brought to me. After I finished dinner, I was alone and feeling rather lonesome.

A White-Robed Visitor

Then I heard footsteps coming down the corridor toward my room. I looked toward the door to see who it was, because it was only 6:30—too early for visitors. Someone dressed in white came through the door, and at first I supposed it was a nurse.

As I looked closer, I saw it was Jesus! It seemed as if the hair on my head stood on end. Cold chill bumps popped out all over my body, and I couldn't say a word.

Jesus approached my bed and sat down on a chair. He was robed in white and wore some sort of sandals. (When I had seen Him before, His feet had been bare.)

The Lord began His conversation with me by saying, "I told you in the automobile the other night as you approached the hospital that your arm was not broken, and you have since learned that this is true. I also told you I would talk to you about this later."

Someone might ask how the Lord told me this. While riding along in the car, I had heard the Lord speak so clearly that I had thought everyone else in the car had heard Him, too. In fact, I had asked, "Did you hear that?" But no one else had heard anything.

In the Old Testament we read the expression over and over, *"the word of the Lord came to me, saying . . ."* (Jer. 2:1). Or, *"the word of the Lord came unto him, saying . . ."* (1 Kings 17:2). This Word certainly wasn't audible, because if it had been an audible voice like a human voice, everyone present would have heard it, and the prophet would not have had to tell the people what the Lord said. But the Word wasn't audible—it came to the prophet's spirit from the Spirit of God, the Holy Spirit. (It is so real, it just seems audible at the time.)

In my hospital room, the Lord reminded me of what He had told me in the car on the way to the hospital. "I told you that your arm was not broken, but that you had knocked your elbow out of place and had a slight fracture," He said. "I also told you this was the devil's work, but it would all work out to my glory and your good."

I replied, "Yes, Lord, and I haven't worried about it for a minute, because I know what You told me. In fact, I've been having a glorious time in the Lord."

Perfect vs. Permissive Will

"You are to be commended for taking me at My Word," Jesus continued. "Now I want to say this to you: This has happened to you not because it was My perfect will for you—because it is not My will at all; this has happened to you because you got out of My perfect will into my permissive will."

He reminded me of the Scripture, *"And be not conformed to this world: but be ye transformed by the renewing of your mind, that ye may prove what is that good, and acceptable, and perfect, will of God "* (Rom. 12:2). I once read a translation of this verse which read, "that you may prove what is that good, and permissive, and perfect will of God."

The Lord explained that He permits people to do things that aren't expressly His will. For example, He said, "It wasn't My will that Israel have a king, and I told them so. But they wanted to be like other nations." (They kept clamoring for a king, so God permitted them to have a king.)

"Some time ago when you preached to a convention of ministers, you stated that your ministry was that of a teacher and a prophet. You got into trouble because you reversed the order of your ministry, putting your teaching ministry first and your prophetic ministry second. When you did that, you got out of *My perfect* will and into *My permissive will,* thus opening the door for the devil to attack you.

"You might ask why, if I knew you were going to fall and hurt your arm, I didn't prevent it. I could have, of course, but I didn't want to. And instead of being angry with Me for not preventing it, you should be glad I allowed it to happen. If I hadn't permitted Satan to do this to arrest your attention, you would not have lived past the age of 55, because you would have continued in my permissive will instead of my perfect will.

"This is the third time I have had to speak to you about this. For this reason, I am going to let you wear your arm in a cast and then in a sling for a little while. I will speed up the healing process, however, so you will not be disabled as long as the doctor has said would be necessary." Then Jesus told me the exact day I would get out of the cast.

He went on to say, "You have enjoyed divine health for 25 years. Even now you are not sick. But," He said, "you have been out of My perfect will for two years and have been walking only in My permissive will."

(More than fifty years have now passed since I was healed as a teenager. The Lord has kept me from sickness and has given me divine health all these years. Hurting my arm was the only accident I have had in all that time.)

Although I had been anointed by the Holy Spirit for the ministries of a prophet and a teacher, I had been putting my teaching ministry first because teaching is my natural preference. I also had seen a great need for Bible teaching, and, of course, pastors had encouraged my teaching ability. But the Lord told me in this vision that I was going to have to reverse it and put my prophet's ministry first.

I realized this accident was not caused by the Lord. He merely permitted it. John 10:10 says, *"The thief cometh not, but for to steal, and to kill, and to destroy: I am come that they might have life, and that they might have it more abundantly."* The one who steals and destroys is the enemy. The Lord doesn't *commission* it, although when man opens a door to the devil, He may *permit* it.

For example, God didn't cause Job's children to be killed or his flocks stolen. God didn't cause the thieves to rob him or the fire to burn his crops. God didn't smite his body with boils. The devil did it. Actually, *Job* gave Satan permission by opening the door to him through fear. God only allowed Satan to do what *Job* had already permitted through the open door of fear (Job 1:5).

In order to get my attention and to bring about my complete submission and obedience to His perfect will, God had allowed this calamity to come into my life. Jesus said to me, "It is my perfect will that men and women enjoy divine healing and divine health, but many are like you and are living only in My permissive will. For that reason, difficulties have been permitted to come their way.

"Others are weak in faith. Their faith is not strong enough to appropriate the healing that belongs to them. Some don't even know what belongs to them. Always pray for people who are sick and in hospitals and are under doctors' care that I will speed up the healing process, because I will do that for you."

Thirteen days later I went back to the doctor to have my cast changed. When it was removed, the doctor looked at my arm in amazement and said, "I have never seen an arm heal so rapidly." Normally it would have taken four weeks for my arm to heal properly.

The doctor had told my wife that I would never be able to touch my shoulder with that arm; however, I can. The Lord told me as He sat there by my hospital bed that He would restore 99 percent of the use of that arm. He said He was going to leave that one percent disability to remind me not to disobey Him again, but to use the ministry He had given me. (My arm gives me only the slightest amount of trouble. No one can ever tell that anything is wrong, and most of the time I have no difficulty with it.)

Healing Promises to Israel

As the Lord continued to speak to me in the vision, He talked to me about the healing ministry, divine healing, and divine health. He reminded me of His promises to Israel concerning healing. Actually, God made a covenant of healing with Israel.

EXODUS 15:26
26 If thou wilt diligently hearken to the voice of the Lord thy God, and wilt do that which is right in his sight, and wilt give ear to his commandments, and keep all his statutes, I will put [permit] none of these diseases upon thee, which I have brought upon the Egyptians: for I am the Lord that healeth thee.

DEUTERONOMY 7:15
15 And the Lord will take away from thee all sickness.

EXODUS 23:26
26 . . . the number of thy days I will fulfil.

The Lord explained, "Israel was not born again; they were not the Church in the same sense you are. You have become children of God—actually the sons of God:

1 JOHN 3:1–2
1   Behold, what manner of love the Father hath bestowed upon us, that we should be called the sons of God.
2   Beloved, now are we the sons of God.

JOHN 1:12
12 But as many as received him, to them gave he power to become the sons of God, even to them that believe on his name.

"The Israelites were not my sons; they were my servants," Jesus said. "And if it was not My will that My *servants* should be sick, certainly it is not My will that My *sons* should be sick. I have provided healing for them."

The Prophet's Ministry

Jesus continued, "I am going to talk to you now about the prophet's ministry. You have missed it and have been only in My permissive will because you have reversed the order of your ministry by putting the teaching ministry first and the prophet's ministry second. Did you ever notice in my Word that everywhere ministry is mentioned, the prophet's ministry is mentioned *first* and the teaching ministry second?

EPHESIANS 4:8,11–12
8 Wherefore he saith, When he ascended up on high, he led captivity captive, and gave gifts unto men . . .
11 And he gave some, apostles; and some, prophets; and some, evangelists; and some, pastors and teachers;
12 For the perfecting of the saints, for the work of the ministry, for the edifying of the body of Christ.

"These are the ministry gifts Paul said God gave to men. And He gave them for this purpose: *'For the perfecting of the saints, for the work of the ministry, for the edifying of the body of Christ.'*[1]

"Notice the order. Apostles are mentioned first. There are some who say that there were only the 12 original apostles. However, there are 23 individuals in the New Testament who are called apostles. The Greek word for 'apostle,' *apostolos,* means 'a sent one.'

"Even Paul himself was not an apostle in the sense of being one of the original 12, for he was not with them from the beginning of My earthly ministry. Judas was one of the 12 original apostles, but after the betrayal, he went out and hanged himself and was replaced by Matthias. This made Matthias the thirteenth apostle.

" *'Which when the apostles, Barnabas and Paul . . .'* (Acts 14:14). Notice that according to this verse, Barnabas was just as much an apostle as Paul was, making them the fourteenth and fifteenth apostles.

"In Galatians we read that Paul said, *'Neither went I up to Jerusalem to them which were apostles before me; but I went into Arabia, and returned again unto Damascus. Then after three years I went up to Jerusalem to see Peter, and abode with him fifteen days. But other of the apostles saw I none, save James the Lord's brother'* (Gal. 1:17-19). [2]

"Here Paul calls James an apostle, although he was not one of the original 12. James was sent to be the head of the Church of Jerusalem. Paul calls him an apostle because he was a 'sent one.' This makes James the sixteenth apostle mentioned in the Scriptures.

"In Romans Paul wrote, *'Salute Andronicus and Junia, my kinsmen, and my fellow prisoners, who are of note among the apostles, who also were in Christ before me'* (Rom. 16:7). Therefore, Andronicus and Junia were apostles seventeen and eighteen.

"Paul began his first epistle to the Thessalonians, *'Paul, and Silvanus, and Timotheus, unto the church of the Thessalonians. . . .'* Then writing in the second chapter, he refers to the three of them as the apostles of Christ (v. 6). This would make these [latter two] men apostles nineteen and twenty.

"In Second Corinthians 8:23, two unnamed brethren are called apostles, raising the number to 22.

"In Philippians Paul said, *'Yet I supposed it necessary to send to you Epaphroditus, my brother, and companion in labour, and fellow soldier, but your messenger, and he that ministered to my wants'* (Phil. 2:25). The Greek word used in this text for 'messenger' is the same one that is translated 'apostle' elsewhere. Therefore, this makes 23 apostles mentioned in the New Testament."

We can see from this that a person can be a 'sent one' or a messenger of the Church and can be correctly called an apostle of the Church. Smith Wigglesworth was called an apostle of faith. When Christ calls and sends someone, he is an apostle of Christ.

The Place of the Missionary

There is no mention of missionaries among the ministry gifts listed in Ephesians 4:11: *"And he gave some, apostles; and some, prophets; and some, evangelists; and some, pastors and teachers."* In fact, the word "missionary" is not found in the New Testament!

The ministry of a missionary is involved in the calling of an apostle. It is a *ministry,* but not necessarily an *office.* For example, if someone were called by the Holy Spirit to be a missionary to Africa, a missionary committee might send him out, but if he were really sent out by the Holy Spirit, he would be an apostle to the people of Africa.

As Jesus pointed out to me in the vision, neither Paul nor Barnabas was an *apostle* to begin with:

ACTS 13:1

1 Now there were in the church that was at Antioch certain prophets and teachers; as Barnabas, and Simeon that was called Niger, and Lucius of Cyrene, and Manaen, which had been brought up with Herod the tetrarch, and Saul.

All five of these men were prophets and/or teachers. Saul and Barnabas are mentioned here, but they are called prophets and teachers, not apostles. We do know that Paul was a prophet and a teacher, and we are told that Barnabas was a teacher. Later they became apostles.

ACTS 13:–4

2 As they ministered to the Lord, and fasted, the Holy Ghost said, Separate me Barnabas and Saul for the work whereunto I have called them.

3 And when they had fasted and prayed, and laid their hands on them, they sent them away.

4 So they, being sent forth by the Holy Ghost, departed.

In other words, Paul and Barnabas were "sent ones," or apostles. The next chapter in the Book of Acts tells us, *"Which when the apostles, Barnabas and Paul . . ."* (Acts 14:14). Barnabas was called an apostle because he was a "sent one" or apostle to the Gentiles as much as Paul was.

The Lord discussed these things with me in the vision to show me that the ministries of the apostle and prophet are still for us today. In dealing with me about the prophet's ministry coming first, He pointed out that the prophet's ministry is listed before the teaching ministry in the Scriptures because Paul listed them *in the order of their importance in the establishment and development of the Early Church:* apostles, prophets, evangelists, pastors, and teachers.[3]

Furthermore, in Acts 13:1, where it mentions the ministers who were praying at the Church in Antioch, it doesn't say "teachers and prophets"; it says "prophets and teachers," and goes on to list them.

As Jesus sat in the chair by my hospital bed, He pointed out the following Scripture to me:

1 CORINTHIANS 12:27–30

27 Now ye are the body of Christ, and members in particular.

28 And God hath set some in the church, first apostles, secondarily prophets, thirdly teachers, after that miracles, then gifts of healings, helps, governments, diversities of tongues.

29 Are all apostles? are all prophets? are all teachers? are all workers of miracles?

30 Have all the gifts of healing? do all speak with tongues? do all interpret?

He said, "Here again, Paul was talking about ministry gifts, not spiritual gifts. Notice, too, that the prophet's ministry is again listed before the teaching ministry. Every time these two gifts are mentioned, the prophet's ministry is mentioned first."

Jesus went on to talk to me about the ministry of the prophet, explaining that a prophet is one who has visions and revelations; things are revealed to him.

In the Old Testament, a prophet was called a "seer" because he saw and knew things supernaturally. By definition, a prophet is one who sees and knows things supernaturally because he has at least two of the revelation gifts plus the gift of prophecy operating in his life and ministry. This constitutes the office of a prophet.

1 CORINTHIANS 14:29–30

29 Let the prophets speak two or three, and let the other judge.

30 If any thing be revealed to another that sitteth by, let the first hold his peace.

Notice in Acts 13:1 that Paul is called a prophet and teacher. Paul said he was taught the Gospel by revelation of Jesus Christ (Eph. 3:3). It came to Paul by revelation; man didn't teach it to him (Gal. 1:12).

It should be noted that one does not begin in the ministry as a prophet. To stand in the office of a prophet, one is first of all a minister of the Gospel separated and called to the ministry with the calling of God upon his life.

He is first and foremost a preacher or a teacher of the Word or a preacher and a teacher of the Word. Second, he must have at least two of the revelation gifts as well as the gift of prophecy operating in his ministry on a continual basis.

The revelation gifts, Jesus pointed out to me, are the word of wisdom, the word of knowledge, and the gift of discerning of spirits.

After I received the baptism of the Holy Spirit, the word of knowledge immediately began to operate in my life on a consistent basis. When I am in the Spirit, the gift of discerning of spirits is also in operation.

Therefore, the word of knowledge and the discerning of spirits plus prophecy are operating in my ministry when I am in the Spirit. This constitutes the office of a prophet.

Any layman may occasionally receive a word of knowledge. The spiritual gift of the word of knowledge is a supernatural revelation by the Holy Spirit of certain facts in the mind of God. God knows everything, but He doesn't reveal everything He knows; He just gives a person a "word" of knowledge. A word is a fragmentary part of a sentence. God gives an individual what He wants him to know at the time—just part of the knowledge He has—and it is given by the Holy Spirit.

Jesus pointed this out to me as He sat by my bedside and spoke to me in this 1959 vision. He said that any Spirit-filled person, whether prophet, minister, or layman, occasionally may have a word of knowledge as he needs it, but having a occasional word of knowledge doesn't make a person a prophet.

The layman isn't called to the five-fold ministry, so he couldn't be a prophet. The minister may be called as an evangelist or a pastor, but he couldn't be called a prophet either simply because he has an occasional word of knowledge to help someone.

To constitute the prophet's office there has to be a continued manifestation of at least two of the revelation gifts plus prophecy.

The Gifts Operated in the Old Testament

Jesus further pointed out to me that all of the gifts except tongues and interpretation of tongues were in operation in the Old Testament. "Tongues," He said, "are exclusive with this dispensation."

Old Testament prophets knew things supernaturally. One example of this is found in Second Kings chapter 5. When Naaman, a captain in the army of the king of Syria, was healed of leprosy after dipping seven times in the River Jordan as commanded by the Prophet Elisha, Naaman offered Elisha much silver and gold. Elisha, however, refused to accept Naaman's money because he realized that Naaman was trying to "pay" for his healing, and it cannot be purchased; healing is a gift from God.

Elisha had a servant named Gehazi, who went after Naaman, telling him that two young prophets had come to see Elisha. Gehazi told Naaman that although Elisha wouldn't take anything for himself, Elisha had said it would be all right for Gehazi to take some talents of silver and gold and some changes of raiment for these young prophets. Naaman was so thrilled and thankful for his healing that he gave Gehazi twice as much as he had asked for.

Gehazi was lying, of course. He had made up the story about the prophets. He took Naaman's gifts and hid them for his own use. Then when he went into the presence of Elisha, and the prophet asked him where he'd been, Gehazi lied and said, "Nowhere."

Elisha replied, *"Went not mine heart with thee, when the man turned again from his chariot to meet thee?"* (2 Kings 5:26). Elisha knew the truth in his spirit. This had to be a supernatural revelation. It was the operation of the word of knowledge in the office of the prophet.

Many people think that if one has this ministry, he can automatically tell everything about everybody, but that's not so. We can't turn Spiritual gifts on and off as we wish; these gifts operate only as the Lord wills.

Gehazi was with the prophet all the time and knew that Elisha didn't know everything all the time. Therefore, Gehazi probably thought he could get by with his deceit.

People often write me wanting me to tell them what is wrong with them. I can't push a button and start operating Spiritual gifts like a tape recorder! Spiritual gifts operate as the Spirit wills and as His anointing comes on me. A person has to be with me in a service when the gift is operating.

This is why I preach about the anointing. When I do, the faith of the congregation rises and the anointing comes on me to minister supernaturally by the gifts of the Spirit. If I could minister this way every night, I would. At times God has had me minister to every person in the crowd, giving me a message for each one. Where the Holy Spirit is in manifestation, anything can happen. I cannot make it happen, however, just because I want it to happen.

Words of Knowledge

Once while I was preaching in Kansas, a minister's wife asked me to pray for her. As she began to share her request with me, the Word of the Lord started coming to me, and I asked her to wait a minute.

I said, "If you tell me your needs before I tell you what the Lord is showing me, you will think I am speaking from my own knowledge. But when God supernaturally shows me a person's need and gives instructions on how to solve their problem, that person knows it is supernatural."

The Lord showed me this woman in a vision. She was very depressed and discouraged. I told her, "I can see you lying in bed with a damp cloth on your head and the shades pulled down because your head hurts so much. Sometimes you remain like this for two or three weeks at a time."

She was amazed that I could know this. Then I gave her the message God gave me. The Lord showed me this woman had committed a sin shortly after she was saved, and ever since that time a deceiving devil had troubled her, repeatedly telling her she had committed the unpardonable sin.

She admitted to me that two years after she was saved she had told a lie, and the devil had tormented her ever since. She told me how a spirit of depression would come upon her for three weeks at a time and she would shut herself up in her room with a cool, damp cloth on her head to ease the pain.

I took authority over this deceiving spirit and commanded him to leave her at once. When I saw her again I learned that she had not been troubled since I ministered to her.

In another city I prayed for a young man who was having epileptic seizures. He was old enough to serve in the Army, but he had been rejected because of the seizures. When he came into the healing line, I knew by the word of knowledge that I had to deal with a evil spirit, so I cast the spirit out of his body in Jesus' Name.

Twelve months later I was back in that church for one service. As I walked through a side door to the platform, my eyes fell on this young man. The Word of the Lord came to me and brought me a word of knowledge, saying, "Last year when you were here, you cast that evil spirit out of his body. For twelve months he has not had an epileptic seizure. However, in the last two weeks he has had three seizures at night while sleeping, and he has been awakened by them.

"The reason for these seizures is that he went to bed fearful and went to sleep afraid."

The Lord then told me that before I preached I should call this young man to the platform and tell him what the Lord had just shown me. He said I should command the evil spirit to leave again. I also was to teach the young man how to resist fear and how to maintain his healing.

As I obeyed the Lord and called the young man to the front, telling him all that the Lord had shown me, he was amazed and he verified what I said.

I told him I was going to cast that evil spirit out of his body, but when I was gone he would be on his own and he would have to resist the devil as we are told to do in James 4:7. Many years have passed since that time, and he has never had another epileptic seizure.

The spiritual gifts that were manifested in my ministry to help this young man were a combination of the gifts of the word of knowledge, discerning of spirits, prophecy, and a teaching ministry that taught him how to resist the devil and maintain what he had.

Have the Ministry Gifts Been Done Away With?

The Word of God tells us that He gave some apostles, some prophets, some evangelists, some pastors, and some teachers. Many will say, "Yes, but these ministry gifts have been done away with now. The only ministries we have today are teachers, pastors, and evangelists. There are no apostles or prophets today."

But notice that Paul made no such distinction. He said that God called some apostles, some prophets, some evangelists, some pastors, and some teachers for the work of the ministry and the edifying of the Body of Christ (Eph. 4:11–12).

Have all the saints been perfected yet? Is there any work of the ministry going on today? Does the Body of Christ still need edifying? If so, all of these ministries and ministry gifts should be in operation. They haven't been done away with.

We need to find our place in God's plan and know what He has called us to do, for He will equip us by His Spirit to stand in the office to which He has called us. We can use the ministry gifts He has given us to minister according to His will, purpose, and plan. Of course, not everyone in the Body of Christ is called to a ministry gift office.

As Jesus sat by my hospital bed in that vision, the Lord reminded me that the word of knowledge immediately began to be manifested in my life from the time I was baptized in the Holy Spirit and spoke in other tongues. The word of knowledge, He pointed out, is supernatural revelation (all the gifts of the Spirit are supernatural). If one of them is supernatural, all of them are supernatural. If the word of knowledge is not a supernatural revelation, the gift of healing would not be supernatural.

Notice, too, that it isn't called "the *gift* of knowledge." It is "the *word* of knowledge." The spiritual gift of the *word of knowledge is* a supernatural revelation by the Holy Spirit concerning people, places, or things in the *present* or in the *past.*

The *word of wisdom,* on the other hand, concerns knowledge of the *future.* The word of wisdom is a supernatural revelation concerning the plan and purpose of God.

When the word of knowledge began to operate in my life, I would know things supernaturally about people, places, and things. Sometimes when I was preaching, a cloud would appear and my eyes would be opened so I could see into the realm of the spirit. I might see as someone in the congregation went to another town and committed a sin. In the vision I would see this person in the other town and I would see the sin that he or she had committed there.

Then I would tell the person about it, but never publicly, because the Bible teaches that only hypocrites should be rebuked publicly. Usually these people are not hypocrites, even though they have sinned. They want to do right. They want to serve God. God shows us these things to help them and to show them how to overcome temptation. We need to realize that this kind of ministry is scriptural and is needed today.

Sometimes the word of knowledge also comes by an inward revelation, a prophecy, or the interpretation of a message in tongues.

Although a person may have a word of wisdom, a word of knowledge, or the discerning of spirits given to him occasionally, that does not make him a prophet.

We see in First Corinthians 14:3, *"But he that prophesieth speaketh unto men to edification, and exhortation, and comfort."* The simple gift of prophecy, therefore, is not given for revelation. Often the utterance a prophet gives will have revelation in it because the prophet has other gifts operating in his ministry, too. But the fact that one prophesies does not make him a prophet.

Many have thought that tongues, interpretation, and prophecy are only for public ministry, but there are more applications for these gifts than that. The simple gift of prophecy can be used as prayer in worship as well as in addressing the congregation or individuals.

In the Book of Psalms we see a number of psalms, songs, and prayers that were spoken in prophecy by the inspiration of the Holy Spirit. The Holy Spirit will help us in our prayer life with tongues, interpretation, and prophecy.

I use tongues and interpretation all the time in my prayer life. Many times I pray in tongues for an hour or so, and then I pray the interpretation in English. In this way, my mind is edified. If I prayed only in tongues, my spirit would be edified, but my mind would be unfruitful. First Corinthians 14:4 says, *"He that speaketh in an unknown tongue edifieth himself* [or his spirit]."

I have prayed as long as six hours a day in tongues and then prayed the interpretation in English. At other times I have used prophecy entirely.

None of this comes from my own mind. I pray in English by a supernatural utterance given by the Holy Spirit. It is a greater blessing to use prophecy in prayer. It lifts one higher than anything else, because prophecy carries greater inspiration than tongues.

Praying in this manner is not limited to ministers. All Spirit-filled Christians can do it. But as I have said, praying in tongues and interpretation or praying with prophecy would not in itself make the individual a prophet.

The Lord taught me all of these things as He sat beside my hospital bed that evening. I'm merely summing them up here in my own words. He also taught me about visions.

Types of Visions

First there is what the Lord called a *spiritual vision,* in which a person has a vision in his spirit, or he sees something in his spirit. This lowest type of vision and the highest type of revelation are very similar.

An example of a spiritual vision is Paul's experience on the road to Damascus. Paul was headed for Damascus, determined to persecute the Christians, when suddenly a light brighter than the noonday sun shone around him, and Paul, then known as Saul, heard a voice saying to him, *"Saul, Saul, why persecutest thou me? And he said, Who art thou, Lord ? And the Lord said, I am Jesus whom thou persecutest."* (Acts 9:4–5).

When relating this experience, Paul said that when this happened, his eyes were shut: *"And Saul arose from the earth; and when his eyes were opened, he saw no man."* (Acts 9:8). Paul didn't see the Lord with his physical eyes; he saw in the spirit realm with the eyes of his spirit.

Also in Acts 9, we see that the Lord spoke to Ananias, who was a layman in the city of Damascus. The Lord told Ananias to go to the street called Straight and inquire for Saul.

ACTS 9:11–12, 17

11 Arise, and go into the street which is called Straight, and enquire . . . for one called Saul of Tarsus: for, behold, he prayeth,

12 And hath seen in a vision a man named Ananias coming in, and putting his hand on him, that he might receive his sight.

17 And Ananias went his way, and entered into the house; and putting his hands on him said, Brother Saul, the Lord, even Jesus, that appeared unto thee in the way as thou camest, hath sent me, that thou mightest receive thy sight, and be filled with the Holy Ghost.

So we see that Jesus appeared to Saul, even though Saul's physical eyes were blinded. This was a spiritual vision. Saul saw Jesus with the eyes of his spirit. This is the first and *lowest* type of a vision.

Jesus pointed out to me that the *second* highest type of vision is when one falls into a *trance*. We see an example of this type of vision when Paul went to Jerusalem the first time. Notice that Paul says he was in a trance.

ACTS 22:17–18
17 And it came to pass, that, when I was come again to Jerusalem, even while I prayed in the temple, I was in a trance;

18 And saw him [Jesus] saying unto me, Make haste, and get thee quickly out of Jerusalem: for they will not receive thy testimony concerning me.

When one falls into a trance, his physical senses are suspended for the moment. He is not aware of where he is or of anything that contacts the physical realm. He is not unconscious—he is just more conscious of spiritual things than he is of physical things.

Acts chapter 10 relates the story of Peter's vision in which the Lord told him to take the Gospel to the Gentiles. Peter went up on a housetop to pray and there he *"fell into a trance"* (v. 10) and saw Heaven opened. He was seeing and hearing in the spirit realm.

So we see from the Bible that both Peter and Paul fell into trances and saw into the spirit realm. A trance, then, is the second highest type of vision.

The *third* type of vision is actually the *highest* type. It is called an *open vision*. When this happens, one's physical senses are not suspended; his physical eyes are not closed. He possesses all of his physical capabilities, yet he still sees and hears in the realm of the spirit.

This is the kind of vision I had when I saw Jesus walk into my hospital room. In an open vision *I heard* His footsteps. I *saw* Him enter my room just as plainly as any man I have ever seen in my life. I *saw* Him sit down beside my bed. I *heard* His voice as plainly as any man's voice I have ever heard in my life.

When the Lord dealt with me concerning my ministry and showed me about the revelation gifts that operate in my life, He spoke to me concerning prophets in the Old Testament who were called "seers." They knew and saw things supernaturally.

The Lord reminded me of the time when Saul as a young boy was out looking for some donkeys that had strayed (1 Samuel 9). When Saul inquired about them, someone suggested he go to the Prophet Samuel and ask him where to find his father's donkeys, because Samuel would know where they were. Saul did go to the prophet, and Samuel told him the donkeys had been found three days before, and now people were out looking for Saul. Samuel knew this supernaturally.

Samuel also asked Saul to wait, because he had a word of wisdom for him concerning God's plan for his life. Samuel then anointed Saul to be the first king of Israel.

Certainly Samuel didn't know the whereabouts of every stray donkey in Israel—there could have been many stray donkeys at that time. But God had a purpose in revealing this to Samuel at that particular time, because it concerned Israel's future king (1 Sam. 9:20).

One time I stopped to visit a minister at the site where he was building a new church. After he had shown me around, we said goodbye and got into our cars to leave. As I was getting into my car, the Word of the Lord came unto me, saying that I should tell this minister that he wasn't going to live much longer unless he corrected himself in three things: his diet, his finances, and his lack of love for the brethren.

I stepped out of my car to go tell him this, but someone else walked up to his car just then and began to talk to him. I sat back down and began to reason with myself. I knew he probably wouldn't take this advice from me. He certainly didn't walk in love toward the brethren, so he probably would slap my face.

As I sat there talking myself out of it, this minister left the site without my telling him what the Lord had shown me. That was the last time I saw him. Three years later he died.

The New Testament talks about the ministry gifts, including the office of the prophet (Eph.4:11; 1 Cor. 12:28). The prophet's ministry is scriptural. First Corinthians 12:28 says that *God* has set these ministries in the Church.

First Corinthians 14 also talks about the prophet speaking and about tongues and interpretation:

1 CORINTHIANS 14:27–30

27 If any man speak in an unknown tongue, let it be by two, or at the most by three, and that by course; and let one interpret.

28 But if there be no interpreter, let him keep silence in the church; and let him speak to himself, and to God.

29 Let the prophets speak two or three, and let the other judge.

30 If any thing be revealed to another that sitteth by, let the first hold his peace.

Most Full Gospel or Charismatic churches will permit tongues and interpretation in their services, but many shy away from the prophet's ministry. However, we have just seen all of these manifestations of the Spirit listed in the same chapter of the Bible with the office of the prophet. If one is omitted, the other should be too.

When the Lord dealt with me concerning the prophet's ministry, He said that if a church wouldn't accept my ministry, I should go my way and shake the dust off my feet against them, so to speak. He told me time is short, and His work must be done quickly in these last days.

Quoting First Peter 4 Jesus said, *"Judgment must begin at the house of God . . . And if the righteous scarcely be saved, where shall the ungodly and the sinner appear?"* (vv. 17,18).

He went on to say that if a church wouldn't accept the ministry of a prophet, they wouldn't accept His Word either. He added that if a pastor wouldn't accept this message, judgment would come upon him.

The Lord said that if He gave me a message or a revelation for a pastor, I should deliver it; and if He gave me a message for a church or an individual, I should deliver it. Some do not believe that personal prophecy is scriptural. They do not believe that a prophet may have a message for an individual. This is what Luke has to say, however, in Acts 21:

ACTS 21:8–11
8   And the next day we that were of Paul's company departed, and came unto Caesarea: and we entered into the house of Philip the evangelist, which was one of the seven; and abode with him.

9   And the same man had four daughters, virgins, which did prophesy.

10 And as we tarried there many days, there came down from Judaea a certain prophet, named Agabus.

11 And when he was come unto us, he took Paul's girdle, and bound his own hands and feet, and said, Thus saith the Holy Ghost, So shall the Jews at Jerusalem bind the man that owneth this girdle, and shall deliver him into the hands of the Gentiles.

One phase of the prophet's ministry is that he speaks for God. In the Scripture quoted above, Agabus didn't tell Paul not to go to Jerusalem; he merely told him what would happen there, and it came to pass.

By the word of wisdom operating through prophecy, a prophet many times has the ability to help people and to prepare them for things that are ahead. Many times God has shown me things along this line that have blessed and helped individuals. We need this kind of manifestation of the Spirit today.

The Lord said to me, "If I give you a message for an individual, a church, or a pastor, and they don't accept it, you will not be responsible. They will be responsible. There will be ministers who won't accept it and who will fall dead in the pulpit."

I say this with reluctance, but this actually happened in one place where I preached. Two weeks from the day I closed the meeting, the pastor fell dead in the pulpit. When I left that church, I left crying.

I told the pastor in the next church where I went to hold a meeting, "That man will fall dead in the pulpit." And just a short time later he did. Why? Because he didn't accept the message God's Spirit gave me to give him.

Some people think we don't need a prophet's ministry in the New Testament Dispensation because we all have the Holy Spirit (we have a measure of the Holy Spirit when we are born again).

The Lord pointed out to me that in Old Testament days, although the laity did not have the Holy Spirit, the Holy Spirit came upon priests, prophets, and kings, to anoint them to stand in their respective offices. And even though the Holy Spirit came upon kings and priests, they still went to the prophets for guidance. *And under the New Covenant, if one has the Holy Spirit, that doesn't mean he has the revelation gifts in operation,* as I pointed out before. However, under the New Covenant, believers are to be led by the Holy Spirit in their recreated human spirit (Rom. 8:14,16).

As the Lord continued to speak with me concerning the prophet's ministry, He reminded me that the day before my accident I had received a letter inviting me for a meeting at a large church. Although I had made no demands for salary, they had promised me a generous offering if I would come to their church. At that particular time, I needed the money very badly.

I had decided to write this pastor and tell him I would come to his church. (If we are not careful, sometimes we will do things for convenience's sake.) But every time I thought about it, I had a dead feeling in my spirit. Later I realized this was the Holy Spirit cautioning me not to go. It was a "stop sign" He had put in my spirit. The Lord didn't want me to go to that church because the pastor wouldn't have accepted my ministry. I would have been wasting my time. As the Lord continued to speak with me, He said, "I am telling you not to go to that church."

The Lord then reminded me of an invitation I had received from a small church whose pastor had asked me to come if the Lord ever led me to. I had almost forgotten about his invitation, but at different times when I was praying, that invitation would come to my mind. When I thought about going to that church, I would have a good feeling, like a green light in my spirit, urging me to go. The Lord told me that was an inward witness. He said we are not led by a prophet's ministry; we are generally led by the Holy Spirit through an inward witness. And the inward witness is something every believer can have.

As the Lord sat there by my bed, He said, "If you will learn to follow this inward witness, I will help you in all the affairs of your life. If My children will listen to me, I will make them wealthy. I am not opposed to their being rich; I am only opposed to their being covetous."

I have learned to follow that inward witness, and it has been a great blessing to me in every area of life.

One time I was praying with a pastor about a certain decision he needed to make. He hadn't told me exactly what he wanted prayer for, but as we were praying together, I began to speak out a psalm that was a message to him. It told him what he had been thinking and what he was waiting for. This message repeated word for word what he had just told his wife. He had a witness in his heart, but didn't know for certain if he should proceed. This message was the confirmation he needed. It lifted a great burden from him.

As Jesus finished His conversation with me that evening in my hospital room, He said, "Be faithful. Fulfill your ministry, for the time is short!"

Then He got up from the chair, walked around the foot of the bed to the door, opened it, and stepped outside. Leaving the door slightly ajar, He walked down the hall.

I heard His footsteps fade away down the corridor just as I had heard Him approaching nearly an hour and a half earlier.

---

[1] For a complete study of this subject, see Rev. Hagin's study guide, *The Ministry Gifts*.

[2] Ibid.

[3] For further study on the subject of apostles and prophets, see Rev. Hagin's book, *He Gave Gifts Unto Men: A Biblical Perspective of Apostles, Prophets, and Pastors*.

Chapter 8

The River of Praise

The Lord appeared to me the seventh time in December 1962 while I was conducting a meeting in Houston, Texas. On the night of December 12, I was telling the people how the Lord had appeared to me in my first vision back in 1950.

As I related some of the things the Lord had told me in that vision, I began to understand more clearly what He had meant by some of those statements, and I also saw where I had failed to obey Him completely.

Immediately I fell on my knees behind the pulpit. I began to cry and say, "Lord, forgive me. I have not obeyed You fully." As I knelt there, I fell into a trance such as Peter did on the house-top, when he had the vision of the sheet being let down from Heaven by the four corners (Acts 10). By this method God led Peter to bring the Gentiles into the Kingdom of God.

The Vision of the Garden

While I was in this trance, I saw a beautiful flower garden. It seemed to be a square garden with a white picket fence around it. It was overgrown with flowers. Climbing roses covered the fence in such profusion that it almost appeared to be a fence made entirely of flowers. Inside the garden was a mass of flowers in full bloom. An arbor covered with climbing flowers stood in the middle of the garden.

This sight was so glorious it is absolutely indescribable. There are no words which could tell of its beauty. Such an aroma went up from these flowers that the fragrance seemed to be multiplied a hundredfold, forming a cloud of incense.

I walked up to the garden from the east, and when I reached the gate, Jesus was there to open it for me. He stretched out His right hand, and, taking my right hand in His, He pulled me through the gate into the garden. Then with His left hand He closed the gate.

He took me down a walkway through the middle of the garden to the arbor. He drew me under the arbor. I saw two white marble seats, one on either side of the arbor. Jesus sat down and invited me to sit down on the seat on the south side of the arbor.

As I looked at Him, I could see to the west of the garden. I asked, "What does this mean? What are all these flowers? What do they represent? I have never seen any place like this in all of my life or smelled any fragrance so magnificent!"

The River of People

To the west I saw flowing into the garden what looked like a river. It narrowed where it came into the garden. Then it seemed to become wider and wider, rising into the sky. It must have been 50 feet wide or more. The river appeared to be pouring tons of water into the garden.

Then the water changed and ceased to be water. Instead of a river of water, it was a river of people! I saw men with silk top hats and long-tailed coats and women in evening gowns. I saw businessmen in smartly tailored suits. I saw laborers and housewives with their work clothes and aprons on. I saw people of all sorts—all of them singing praises as they flowed into the garden.

Then the Lord said to me, "These people whom you see flowing like a river into this garden are what you call 'denominational people' or denominations other than Full Gospel. In this day I am visiting hungry hearts everywhere. Wherever I find hearts that are open to Me, in whatever church they may be, I will visit them in this hour. I also will visit places you never would have thought I would visit—not only what you call 'denominational churches,' but I also will visit other religions where hearts are hungry and open to Me. I will bring them into a full salvation and into the baptism of the Holy Spirit.

"This river is all these people who will be called in these last days and who will flow as one and will come together as one. The beautiful aroma of these flowers is the praise of these people ascending into Heaven, even as the incense of old ascended unto Me."

My Role Outlined

The Lord continued, "You must play a part in this. You will work with these people in the various denominations. You will minister to Full Gospel people to help them be prepared for my coming. I will show you how and what to do."

Then He took my hand as I stood up, and walked with me back to the gate. He opened it with His left hand, still holding my right hand in His. I went through the gate and then He closed it behind me. As I stood just outside the gate, the vision disappeared.

I came to myself and realized I was on my face behind the pulpit. I arose and told the people what I had seen, and it blessed and inspired all of us.

We have seen this vision come to pass to some extent since 1962, but we have not seen the fullness of it yet. That river is still flowing. There are many who still shall come to this river of God, shall drink of it, and shall walk in the fullness of the Spirit. They shall come from every church and from every country. We are seeing this fulfilled, and we will continue to see it fulfilled in the days that are just before us.

Chapter 9

The Angel's Message

The eighth time I saw the Lord—or the next "divinely granted appearance" as *The Amplified Bible* puts it—was in August 1963. It was primarily for my own benefit; however, because it does involve the ministry, I shall relate it here.

At this time we were in an eight-week series of meetings, and during the last three weeks we had set aside two nights a week solely for prayer; there was no preaching. I had told the people that there would be no sermon, only prayer, on those nights, and if they were not coming to pray, not to plan to come to the services. Yet the crowds were as large on those nights as they were on the other nights.

One night as we were all praying (I was kneeling on the platform), Jesus suddenly appeared before me. Again, an angel stood about three feet behind Him. This angel was quite tall; he must have been seven feet tall or more.

Jesus began to talk to me about my ministry. A short time before this, my wife had written me concerning my sister, who had just been told by the doctors that she had cancer. I had been praying for my sister before the Lord appeared to me.

He said, "Your sister will live and not die. There is no danger of immediate death." He said that she would live at least another five years, and she did. (When she died after five years

exactly, she did not die from the condition that existed at that
time; her death was caused by something else.)

Some Angelic Messengers

Every time I looked up at the angel he looked back at me as
if he were about to say something. But then I would look back
to Jesus and the angel wouldn't say anything. Finally I said to
the Lord, "Who is this angel and what does he represent?"

Jesus said, "That's your angel."

"My angel!" I said.

"Yes, don't you know, it is written in My Word where I
said to My disciples, *'Suffer little children, and forbid them
not, to come unto me: for of such is the kingdom of heaven'*
[Matt. 19:14]. Then in another place I said, *'For their angels
do always behold the face of my Father which is in heaven'*
[Matt. 18:10].

"You don't lose your angel just because you grow up," Jesus
said. "He has a message for you," the Lord said. Well, think
about it. Why would we lose our angel just because we grow up.

"But, Lord, You are here. Why can't You deliver the message?" (After all, I wanted to be scriptural. The Holy Spirit is to
be our Guide. He is the One who is to give us guidance as well
as the Word of God. But I wasn't sure about an angel giving me
a message.) I said to Jesus, "You know that I am a real stickler
for the Word."

Jesus said to me, "Didn't you ever read in the Bible where
an angel of the Lord came and awakened Peter when he was
in jail, and in answer to prayer led him out of jail? Don't
you remember that the angel of the Lord appeared to Philip
and gave him directions after that great citywide meeting in
Samaria, telling him to go down by the way of Gaza? And there,
you will remember, the Ethiopian eunuch was converted to
Christianity and carried the Gospel back to Ethiopia.

"Don't you remember that the angel of the Lord appeared to Paul when he was on board the ship on his way to Rome to appeal his case before Caesar? A storm had arisen and all the merchandise on the ship had been thrown overboard in an attempt to save the vessel and its passengers. All hope that they should be saved was gone.

"Then Paul stood and said, *'I exhort you to be of good cheer: for there shall be no loss of any man's life among you, but of the ship. For there stood by me this night the angel of God, whose I am, and whom I serve, Saying, Fear not, Paul; thou must be brought before Caesar: and, lo, God hath given thee all them that sail with thee'"* (Acts 27:22–24). The Lord said, "Didn't the angel give Paul direction? Didn't he have a message for Paul from God?"

The Lord also reminded me of the time when Paul was praying in the Temple in Jerusalem, fell into a trance, and saw Jesus. Jesus told him, *"Make haste, and get thee quickly out of Jerusalem"* (Acts 22:18). Then after Paul was arrested, before appealing his case to Caesar, the Lord appeared to him one night in jail in Jerusalem and told him not to be afraid, for Paul was to bear witness of Jesus' Name before kings and authorities.

So we see that although Jesus had appeared to Paul and had given him words of comfort and direction, the angel of the Lord had also appeared to him and had given Paul direction.

Ministering Spirits

In teaching me about angels, the Lord pointed out the Scripture, *"Are they not all ministering spirits, sent forth to minister for them who shall be heirs of salvation?"* (Heb. 1:14).

I always had thought this verse said, "minister *to* them who shall be heirs of salvation." But the Word says, "minister *for* them." The word "minister" used here carries the thought of to wait on or to serve. For instance, when you go into a restaurant, a waitress comes to minister to you, to wait on you, or to serve you. In other words, she waits for your order.

The Lord said to me, "Angels are ministering spirits who are sent to minister, not just to one, but for all who are heirs of salvation."

Someone might ask, "Well, then why haven't they done anything?" They are waiting for you to give them the order, just as a waitress cannot do anything for you until you give her the order!

The Angel's Message

After the Lord quoted these scriptures from the Word, I repented for my ignorance. I thought I was being a stickler for the Word.

You know, I think many times dear people have been defeated by thinking they were sticklers for the Word, when they were really just being sticklers for what they *thought* the Word said. The Word may have more to say on some subjects than they realized.

So I said to the Lord, "All right, Lord, now I understand." You see, if we're not careful, we can get so conscious of obeying the letter of the Word that we miss the Spirit of the Word and shut the door on God and on the move of the Holy Spirit.

After the angel had delivered his message to me, the Lord said, "Now respond to him."

Then I looked to the angel and asked, "What is it you have to say to me?"

He replied, "I am sent from the Presence of God to tell you not to let So-and-so (and he mentioned a certain man's name) duplicate your tapes, for he has ulterior motives. I am sent with this message to tell you that in four months' time, you'll have in your possession so many thousands of dollars (and he mentioned a certain amount), and you will have enough to set up your own office and make your own tapes.

"Not only will you have this money in four months' time, but other money will come, for my angels are at work now to cause the money to come."

I said, "What do you mean, 'my angels'?"

He said, "I am over a number of angels, and I've got them working now."

Four months later, just like that angel said, I had the money he said I would have. I was able to establish our office and do the work of God without being under bondage to anyone. That was a divinely granted appearance concerning my ministry.

I have since learned to say, "Go, ministering spirits and cause the needed money to come in. In Jesus' Name."

I praise God that He will direct us and guide us today—even by visions when necessary—not as we might will, but as He wills!

Believers aren't to pray and seek for angels to appear to them; the devil might accommodate them. The Bible says, *"For Satan himself is transformed into an angel of light"* (2 Cor. 11:14).

Just stay faithful to God. If God sees fit, a believer may have a divinely granted appearance. If God doesn't, that's fine too. God is the One who grants these things as He wills.

A Sinner's Prayer
to Receive Jesus as Savior

Dear Heavenly Father

I come to You in the Name of Jesus.

Your Word says, *"The one who comes to Me I will by no means cast out"* (John 6:37 NKJV). I know You won't cast me out. You take me in, and I thank You for that.

You said in Your Word, *"Whoever calls on the name of the Lord shall be saved"* (Rom 10:13 NKJV). I am calling on Your Name, and I know You have saved me.

You also said, *"If you confess with your mouth the Lord Jesus and believe in your heart that God has raised Him from the dead, you will be saved. For with the heart one believes unto righteousness, and with the mouth confession is made unto salvation"* (Rom. 10:9–10). I believe in my heart Jesus Christ is the Son of God. I believe He was raised from the dead for my justification. I confess Him as my Lord.

Because Your Word says that *"with the heart one believes unto righteousness"*—and I do believe with my heart—I have now become the righteousness of God in Christ (2 Cor. 5:21). I am now saved!

Thank You Lord!

Signed _____

Date _____

Always on.

For the latest news and information on products,
media, podcasts, study resources, and
special offers, visit us online 24 hours a day.

rhema.org

Rhema

Correspondence Bible School

The Rhema Correspondence Bible School is a home Bible study course that can help you in your everyday life!

This course of study has been designed with you in mind, providing practical teaching on prayer, faith, healing, Spirit-led living, and much more to help you live a victorious Christian life!

Flexible

Enroll any time: choose your topic of study;
study at your own pace!

Affordable

Profitable

"The Lord has blessed me through a Rhema Correspondence Bible School graduate. . . . He witnessed to me 15 years ago, and the Lord delivered me from drugs and alcohol. I was living on the streets and then in somebody's tool shed. Now I lead a victorious and blessed life! I now am a graduate of Rhema Correspondence Bible School too! I own a beautiful home. I have a beautiful wife and two children who also love the Lord. The Lord allows me to preach whenever my pastor is out of town. I am on the board of directors at my church and at the Christian school. Thank you, and God bless you and your ministry!"

—D.J., Lusby, Maryland

"Thank you for continually offering Rhema Correspondence Bible School. The eyes of my understanding have been enlightened greatly through the Word of God through having been enrolled in RCBS. My life has forever been changed."

—M.R., Princeton, N.C.